W9-BYL-550

MORE PRAISE FOR *SALES BLAZERS*

"I have read a lot of sales books in my career and many of them fail to deliver. Sales Blazers concepts are real world, advanced strategies that anyone leading in the trenches needs to know."
—Glenn Seninger, Regional Vice President,
Oracle Corporation

"Great sales professionals who produce superior results have some key characteristics in common. These are chronicled in *Sales Blazers*, which goes to the heart of what successful growth leaders do to create high performance. . . . This is a must-read for any sales professional who wants to achieve breakthrough results."
—Tim Treu, Executive Vice President of Sales,
O.C. Tanner Company

"Perceptive and practical advice delivered in a logical and concise manner. *Sales Blazers* communicates rich content on how to win crucial, complex battles by executing straightforward tactics."
—Clark A. Campbell, author of
The One-Page Project Manager

"I recommend *Sales Blazers* to every business leader, not to just sales professionals. . . . The principles offered in *Sales Blazers* will benefit all leaders who are interested in advancing their personal growth, key metrics, and careers."
—Bryan Wilde, Vice President of
Human Resources, FranklinCovey

"Founded on practice, the patterns of leadership Cook outlines can and will make a significant difference to any firm that values dramatic revenue gains year after year."

—Steve C. Wheelwright, Ph.D., Edsel Bryant Ford
Professor of Business Administration, Emeritus,
Harvard Business School

"From the moment I began reading *Sales Blazers*, I recognized this book was the perfect framework for influencing professional clients with integrity and helping distributors increase their sales. As I read this book, I grew anxious to get it in the hands of my independent salespeople and teams to ramp revenue. This is a critical model for building relationships with new prospects and strengthening relationships throughout the distribution channel. The ending is as compelling as the beginning, and the practical nature of the strategies throughout the book is vividly real."

—Joe Coen, Vice President of Sales, Biomet Orthopedics

"We brought the Sales Blazers method into our sales force, and the strategies made an immediate impact. The strategies clarified several key strides in the minds of our representatives and leaders that will change the way we sell forever."

—Kevin Childs, President of Global Alliances, UCN,
and coauthor of *Interpreting the Voice of the Customer*

SALES
BLAZERS

8 GOAL-SHATTERING STRATEGIES FROM THE WORLD'S TOP SALES LEADERS

MARK COOK

New York   Chicago   San Francisco   Lisbon   London
Madrid   Mexico City   Milan   New Delhi   San Juan
Seoul   Singapore   Sydney   Toronto

The McGraw·Hill Companies

Copyright © 2008 by O.C. Tanner Company. All rights reserved. Printed in the United States of America. Except as permitted under the United States Copyright Act of 1976, no part of this publication may be reproduced or distributed in any form or by any means, or stored in a data base or retrieval system, without the prior written permission of the publisher.

1 2 3 4 5 6 7 8 9 0   DOC/DOC   0 1 4 3 2 1 0 9 8

ISBN 978-0-07-154684-3
MHID 0-07-154684-7

McGraw-Hill books are available at special quantity discounts to use as premiums and sales promotions, or for use in corporate training programs. To contact a representative please visit the Contact Us pages at www.mhprofessional.com.

This book is printed on acid-free paper.

Library of Congress Cataloging-in-Publication Data
Cook, Mark, 1967–
   Sales blazers : 8 goal-shattering strategies from the world's top sales leaders / by Mark Cook.
         p. cm.
   ISBN 0-07-154684-7 (alk. paper)
   1. Sales management.   2. Selling.   I. Title.
HF5438.4.C664   2008
658.85—dc22

                                                                2007044517

Contents

CONTENTS

Foreword

Before recommending a book, I consider four things: the author, the underlying principles, the practicality, and the vision that the book creates for the reader. *Sales Blazers* didn't just pass my four tests, it excels in each of these areas. This book is destined to become a classic and those that adopt it first will grow tremendously as people and as organizations.

First, consider the author. I know Mark's work, but just as important, I know his roots. Mark comes from stock that can be trusted and has always been focused on improving humanity, not just business. Early in Mark's career with FranklinCovey, he showed a focus on growth. He sought out and envisioned opportunities to touch more lives, creating more revenue. He helped expand our few stores into one of the most respected national chains of specialty stores in the world. Mark continued to create business with new catalogs, training, and publishing—

he's a brilliant salesman, a rare leader. He worked directly for my son, Stephen M. R. Covey, early in his career, and my son called him a "proven business builder." Mark has gone on to do the same with a successful technology start-up and now creates new business for O.C. Tanner, an outstanding performance company. You can trust Mark's experience with his strategies.

Second, consider the deeper principles underlying Mark's strategies—removing obstacles, championing human beings, creating actual value, cooperating better, focusing on work's essence, advising others, and celebrating growth. Sure, Mark has presented the newest, freshest differentiators in these areas and gathered them from extraordinary leaders, but these underlying principles are critical for any business success. These underlying principles are what compelled me to introduce this work because these are also principles critical to any human success.

Third, consider the practical nature of the strategies you are about to read. There are millions of books in the world today and few authors have gone to the lengths that Mark has to support his findings in a way that makes them directly applicable to your work, and applicable immediately. It seems business leaders pull new management levers every year in an attempt to create new growth. Likewise sales forces introduce new highly tactical tricks of selling. *Sales Blazers* delivers something new for a sales force or business besides management or tricks. Mark has assembled authentic strategies to grow business, not just this year but for the long term. The strategies are real and enduring—fresh air for an anxious business climate.

Perhaps the most important accomplishment of *Sales Blazers* is that it creates a vision of hope. Throughout the book, highlighting each of the strategies, are brief, dramatic stories of success that inspire belief that growth will happen for you and your company this year and next. Even more important is the vision that Mark creates that growth will come to you as a person by applying these strategies. *Sales Blazers* is not one of a million brief works of entertainment; it is instructive and paints a picture of exactly what needs to be done by you to lead an inspiring year and decade of growth. Enjoy. *Sales Blazers* is one of the most important books you will ever read.

Stephen R. Covey

Acknowledgments

I feel humbled by the list in my mind of all the people who helped this project come to fruition. I could literally type pages itemizing the meaningful contributions of others. I'm deeply grateful to each person I've named below and to those I've mentioned generally. A partial list of champions and partners who invested the most time and passion in this project begins with my dear wife, Annika, each of our boys, and our families for their time, ideas, and unending support. Thank you so very much; you are deservedly loved.

Without the early encouragement, support, and adoption of this project by Kent Murdock, David Sturt, Dave Petersen, Clark Campbell, Tim Treu, and other O.C. Tanner executives and colleagues, this book would be a shadow of what it is. The same is true for the faith expressed by Donya Dickerson and the McGraw-Hill team; thank you so much for your belief, coaching, and expertise in this sales and leadership endeavor.

In any multiyear project there are those people who appear at pivotal moments and have a rare impact. I can't begin to express enough appreciation to William Nelson, Linda Allen, Kevin Salmon, Ty Brown, Ron Pynes, and the Axis41 team, and to those close to me who waded through the very first words put on pages or offered important, early direction. Thank you to Mark Victor Hansen and Stephen M. R. Covey for always showing up for me. Perhaps what I value most in each of you is that you have demonstrated an unwavering faith in this idea—and in me—when the way was still unclear; thank you so very much for shedding some light.

I also acknowledge many, many others—my heroes—some of whom are referenced throughout the book, for exemplifying each strategy and for their willingness to help develop this project over the past several years.

With deep gratitude, I acknowledge my parents, Cal and Nadine, and God for the profound influence they had on my thinking during this process. Thanks to all of you for being champions of people.

The Heroics of Extraordinary Growth

For years, I hunted for sales teams that had blazed through challenges to achieve unprecedented growth rates, outperforming trends and their counterparts. I hoped to find secret leadership strategies for dramatic growth that could be repeated by salespeople at any level to become extraordinary leaders of consultative sales and support efforts. In all my research, of all the winning strategies I encountered, and of all the leaders with whom I worked, one story hit me so hard I couldn't sleep the night I heard it.

Bo Scott's story is nothing short of heroic, a tale of influencing those around him to achieve great sales growth; it embodies every winning strategy I came across. It convinced me that I had found the leadership secrets of extraordinary growth and, more important, that Bo's secrets could be repeated.

It took Bo's young family a couple of years to settle in around his new, busy job as an area sales manager for a multi-billion-dollar company that sells industrial systems. After those two years, he forced an amazing change in growth . . . again. Bo and one of his reps told me the story.

"We came off a year where the team miraculously grew sales 18 percent to just over $50 million," Bo said. "We were second in growth at the company. Other major things were brewing as well. An organizational analysis showed sales needed deeper engineering—an increase in staff of 30 percent. It was the right thing to do, but there was little focus on what it would take.

"You know who's going to have to pay for the new hires, right? Our celebration of the 18 percent came to a screeching halt when we were handed a new quota of 20 percent. This was on top of the $50 million base we'd just created."

Bo recounted how they were also saddled with hiring all the new people. Before everyone was on board, the hiring expenses and distractions were already adding up. Then the real storm hit.

"Our team was being combined with another area, and we had to manage that, too," Bo said. "Then Development announced that key new products would be delayed into next year. We had about as many moving parts as one team could possibly have. During the quota process, Finance changed the way they recognized revenue, which pushed some contracts my area was assigned quota for outside the fiscal year."

He noted that just before these events, the company changed how it rewarded low-churn accounts. Without going into detail, this meant the team would likely break over half the sales relationships they had with customers. The situation seemed crazy compared to what they'd faced the year before. And there was more.

"Finance decided that with the change in revenue recognition, they needed to calculate growth differently," Bo continued. "They compared apples and oranges and tried to tell us that we really only had a goal of 10 percent growth. It seemed crazy because these were smart people. When you measured the same dates this year, compared to the same dates last year, and measured revenue from the exact same accounts, it was nearly a 29 percent growth.

"So not only did we have this huge goal of 29 percent growth, but our finance people weren't even willing to acknowledge it."

It appeared that the team had been handed a quota that hadn't been thought through by the company. It seemed there was even denial on some levels in the organization about a number they couldn't change.

"It was incredibly frustrating to a team which had just come off a heroic year; we were number 2 in growth, achieving 115 percent of our revenue goal," Bo explained.

"All they could say was, 'Look, we're going to find a way to be successful. You're going to have more people soon. You've got a strong team in place. You've got strong products. Yes, we have some delays in new product, but you guys can do it.'

"It was a blind-faith kind of thing. I was sick. There were many moments that I thought, 'I can't with conviction and honesty tell my people, who I've built trust with, that this is going to be easy or that this is even achievable.' My people were already saying, 'We'll start selling for next year.' They didn't believe it was possible."

PROBLEM: LAST YEAR'S BIG SUCCESS IS THIS YEAR'S FIERCEST RIVAL

The first part of Bo's story shows the problem that this book can help you solve: When you are thanked for last year's big success with a raised expectation from the board or a steep quota increase and no new means, you're not alone. Nearly all salespeople and leaders are asked to pull off what feels like a miracle every year, and they have to *lead* clients, reps, support people, or an entire workforce to do it.

A leader's revenue challenge comes in many flavors. Some leaders are asked to increase the trajectory of an already steep revenue chart; some are asked to move modest growth to extraordinary; others are asked to spring life into a flat line.

The task of the revenue-responsible is most serious when, after working harder than ever, sales continue to fall, but the company demands unprecedented growth anyway. The only solution usually offered with an increase in revenue expectations is "work harder," and this often to those already working nearly 24/7.

I knew there had to be a better solution—and that is why I went looking for new answers to accelerating growth.

Reps sometimes think they carry the whole weight of the quota. Dan, a sales vice president for Nova Chemical, explained that the quota pressure goes all the way up the ranks and touches everyone in sales or who supports revenue in any way.

"It's like a chain reaction. Every year there's that moment when revenue expectations are finalized and distributed. Everyone in sales takes a deep breath and wonders how in the world they can possibly pull off their new number. First, the stockholders and board members put pressure on the CEO. Then, top sales leadership gets a turn to wince at the steep goal. Next, channel partners receive a visit and the field leadership feels the heat.

"When frontline leadership hands out quotas to salespeople," continues Dan, "it's the reps' turn for the moment of truth. Some salespeople react with, 'That quota is impossible!' and give 50 reasons why. A rep or two have anxiety attacks they keep to themselves. They don't think about the fact that this same tough moment happens all down the line at every level, not just to them. Last year's big success sure fades fast."

Mandates to accelerate growth are especially difficult when last year's big success included large, once-in-a-lifetime deals.

Kevin, a sales vice president selling select human resource services, explained how the pressure mounts.

"Everything is humming along as well as it can, and two salespeople bring in a couple of large, one-time deals at the same time. The volume and timing are so rare that you know it's only going to happen once in a blue moon; you can't just repeat it next year. But the company expects you to anyway. It's ironic; sometimes last year's big success is this year's fiercest rival."

With all cylinders already firing, leaders like Kevin and Bo describe the upcoming challenge of finding a plan to increase this year's sales. Bo explained, "Our goal was well above $60 million after doing the real math. We got to work, but it took me four months to get myself to a point where I could accept the situation and stop trying to convince people of the insanity of what they were trying to make us do. One of the positive things was that my new VP was the former number 1 revenue leader in the company. He was now on my side, and he validated that my words were not the usual quota complaints. But he also had a positive attitude because, while we inherited his former team's quota too, we now had the combined number 1 and 2 growth teams to help us achieve this insane goal. If it could even happen, it was going to be a fight to the very end. It was time to start thinking. It would take every ounce of leadership we could muster, because all of our people and clients didn't believe yet."

SALES BLAZERS

Sales Blazers get others not only to believe but also to deliver revenue boosts, outperforming trends and counterparts. They accelerate growth to extraordinary rates without relying on groundbreaking ad campaigns, changes in the local economy, or another rep's solo performance. Their change in revenue trajectory is created by one factor above all others—the Sales Blazers' new approach. All salespeople working through less-than-simple, relationship-oriented sales must lead people. Our situations vary from getting a low-level influencer on our side, to leading a prospect's large committee to a close, to leading a virtual team of support and subject-matter experts who don't even report to us, to inspiring a sales force of 100,000 direct reports to deliver unprecedented growth rates; in most every sales situation, our most important challenge is to become extraordinary leaders of those in the flow of commerce. This book is not about replacing your selling steps or about static management; it is about gaining an effective, genuine means of influencing people—leadership that blazes revenue to the highest level.

There is already a mountain of material out there about selling processes and management. What is in short supply is a compilation of leadership strategies that go beyond the basics—advice from all those mentors who've pulled off dramatic growth. The good news is that I found such Sales Blazers in some of the largest organizations in the world: GM, Oracle, Avon, GE Healthcare, Pfizer, Sprint, and other Fortune 500 companies. Observations also came from people who work with over 100 Sales Blazers, who represent other organization sizes, industries, and income brackets.

Identifying Sales Blazers was a difficult process that took years. Companies and loyal salespeople were justifiably wary about identifying their star leaders and strategies. Most required confidentiality. For that reason, last names and some household company names are omitted, but the observations are noted. The research had one objective: Find out what these rare leaders have learned to become the identifiable cause of superior growth.

As you read on, you will see that Sales Blazers create a point at which everything comes together to change the revenue chart. Many are even humble about sharing their successful outcomes. Bo and the other leaders describe their secrets of success in the chapters that follow, but how Bo shared his success is also worthy of note.

"It was an effort above and beyond me," Bo said. "If it was going to happen, it would be impossible for us to achieve this number with just basic selling or management. It would take something extra to force the change in growth. We finished at 105 percent of goal.

> The *difference* between the sales results of Sales Blazers and those of their counterparts was sizable. Remove exceptions like "$6 million increased to $100 million" and isolate cases of solid leadership and the difference was around 5 percent growth for the norm and 31 percent for Sales Blazers (see Figure I.1).

"After 20 years in sales, I've finished as a sales rep at 200 percent of quota and above 150 percent as a district leader. Nothing I've done has meant as much as that 105 percent because of the challenges we faced while hiring 60 percent of the team. We managed to change the wheels on the speeding car without stopping. We started not only in a hole with a heavy quota, but we were also still adding people to the team.

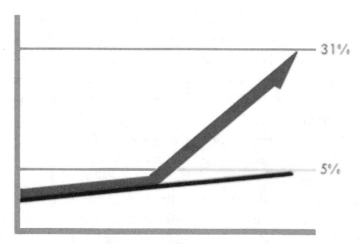

Figure I.1 Sales Blazer Growth

I was just at the point on a heroic team. We made 105 percent of quota—about 35 percent growth."

THE BIG QUESTION

"How did you achieve extraordinary growth?" was the question asked by the Sales Blazer project. The answer would help reveal how some leaders accelerate growth while their counterparts, even at the same companies, lead only small gains.

I asked Bo, "How did you lead 34 percent annual growth right after an award-winning 18 percent?"

Bo's response will increase in clarity and detail in the chapters that follow as we discuss more deeply what we found with him and other Sales Blazers.

"I started by relentlessly protecting people from distraction," he said. "Then it took tremendous one-on-one time with each individual to help them realize this was about something more than the numbers and the money; it was about who they were and what we all could believe was possible.

"We placed some competitive bets early last year. They all had to hit to make it. To pull this off, we had to prepare as partners, not individuals," Bo added.

"Everybody needed clear accountability and rewards that contributed in specific ways to reach the goal. It took more than management. I had to be a better leader; it took a coaching-like effort and constant feedback. And my people gave a heroic commitment to change. Most of all, successes deserved reward, and I made sure that each was rewarded in an individual way."

THE SALES BLAZER METHOD

I organized the secrets of Bo's and other Sales Blazers' strategies into a repeatable framework called the *Sales Blazer Method.* Many successful strategies were found among over 100 Sales Blazers observed, but eight strategies that accelerated team growth were found to be common to all. These strategies reach across internal and field sales teams and work for any size com-

Strategies as differentiators: The eight strategies are leadership differentiators that produced extraordinary results. The observations, combined with universal, repeatable principles, make up each strategy.

pany. To determine the reliability of the observations, they were correlated with actual sales increases. The difference between a Sales Blazer and a mediocre manager is that a Sales Blazer consistently uses all eight of the identified strategies to step up growth.

THE EIGHT LEADERSHIP STRATEGIES
FOR SALES GROWTH

1. Start with a Clean Bill of Health
2. Spark a Performance Pursuit
3. Get the Express Pass
4. Play Your Depth Chart
5. Activate Expectations
6. Coach Like a Professional
7. RSVP Feedback
8. Heighten Reward Potency

Each chapter of this book explores one of the eight strategies. Rather than share piles of observations, I share short quotes, metaphors, key examples, and the expertise of relevant specialists to explain the essence of the findings. This will make it easier for you to understand and repeat each strategy whether you are in the field or at an internal sales desk.

The strategies are stand-alone ideas but they have a natural sequence, and Sales Blazers use all eight strategies in concert. The first three strategies help us *prepare* better, strategies four and five give us a new way to *engage* broad teams, and the final three strategies improve our ability to *lead*. Each strategy builds on the previous one. The sequence of *prepare*, *engage*, and *lead* explains the method as a whole (see Figure I.2).

Figure I.2 Complete Sales Blazers Method

- *Start with a Clean Bill of Health* is a strategy that helps you discover the most severe risks to revenue and address them first so that you don't cancel out any positive steps you are about to take.
- *Spark a Performance Pursuit* involves learning about and motivating each person you work with in a highly productive way.
- *Get the Express Pass* is a strategy for learning about key prospects and competition in a more focused, competitive way.
- *Play Your Depth Chart* is a way to use your new knowledge of people, prospects, and competition to align the team for results.

- *Activate Expectations* is a specific approach for clarifying the work that actually contributes to results.
- *Coach Like a Professional* includes ways to gain respect from other people and increase momentum to maximize each sales situation.
- *RSVP Feedback* provides better feedback for better results.
- *Heighten Reward Potency* is a strategy for celebrating success in a more individual, motivating way.

Keeping performance momentum begins with the individual, whether motivating a prospect, rewarding a rep, or cascading a culture of appreciable growth from the executive level.

The Sales Blazer Method is directed at consultative reps, managers, support people, channel partners, and executives—anyone responsible for leading revenue—for good reason. Significantly bending the sales trend upward requires touching the daily performance of everyone, even prospects. The fastest and most dynamic path to dramatic change is through leadership—a way to reach all the players.

The eight strategies constitute a method for leading others. Salespeople can use the strategies to lead prospects and clients to increased sales. Top leadership can use this method to create leaders out of all the aspiring, middle, and frontline salespeople in the organization. Executives who put these strategies in the hands of leaders organization-wide make a difference in culture, momentum, and the margin of performance, changing the entire company's revenue trajectory. In less formal organizations, individuals whose earnings depend on the sales of those below them can use this leadership method to increase their own incomes. In any case, you will morph the leader–follower relationship into a partnership for individual, team, and company success.

WHO'S GOT THE TIME?

Sales Blazers will guide you through the Sales Blazer Method—differentiators that crescendo the careers of Sales Blazers. The exploration will include some exciting detail and will take a new approach to work you already do.

"The reader better know the fundamentals," as Bo said. These include "having a consistent selling process and momentum in your pipeline, and understanding your value proposition, competition, solution, and customers, plus the other standards of traditional sales.

"The problem is these are things we all work on every year—why would we expect to get a different result? What you describe in *Sales Blazers* takes it to the next level. A person with a base of experience will benefit from the Sales Blazer Method far more than someone coming out of college. People who will spur growth with this are the ones who have at least some experience under their belts, both good and bad, so they can truly appreciate the content and not just try to use it as a step-by-step recipe without a foundation. If they do this, it will impact growth."

In the final chapter you will learn how to put together everything you've learned. I promise that we will arrive at an action plan to lead growth that is completely possible and that takes no more time than you currently spend. The Sales Blazer Method is not a whole new set of tasks; it is a way to rise above the basics. The strategies can be repeated and used as a standard for self-evaluation—a way to decide if you are becoming a Sales Blazer even before you achieve your new growth.

Start with a Clean Bill of Health

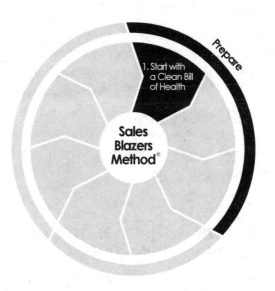

THE STRATEGY

Before you make any big moves, find and remove hidden threats to results—*Start with a Clean Bill of Health.*

> *What we will accomplish in this chapter:* We will look at factors that are common to any sales organization and describe distractions that hamper selling. We will learn how to easily measure for any severe problems, and we will discuss to what degree these weaknesses need to be fixed.

More Than Listening, Less Than a Headhunt

Before making big changes, Sales Blazers say, "Fixing the right small problems can have a tremendous impact on productivity." The first Sales Blazer strategy, *Start with a Clean Bill of Health*, is neither a headhunt to fire people nor a mission to solve every complaint. It's like getting a checkup before running a marathon. The key, as I observed it, is to swiftly find hidden, severe weaknesses in time management, organization, and capabilities and improve them just enough to return focus to selling.

THE PROBLEM: SEVERE WEAKNESS AND SPREADING DISTRACTION

Mediocre businesspeople completely underestimate some problems. A nagging itch that seems normal can, if unchecked, spread into a debilitating condition. The following events, based on several true stories, illustrate how important it is to detect severe problems before jumping into any big endeavor. The names and events have been altered to protect the people involved.

Judy held on to her wheelchair with her new prosthetic hand while her friends pushed her toward the starting line to watch a friend run a marathon. For a former runner, it was a sober moment. One year earlier, after a similar race, Judy had nearly died—but running hadn't been the reason.

In the excitement at registration on the way to the starting line, Judy asked a medical technician to look at a severe bruise and skin infection that had coincidentally started bothering her the previous night. She hadn't paid much attention to the skin problem the night before because she hadn't felt well and was worried about whether she'd be able to race the next morning. The technician she asked had seen similar infections many times and encouraged Judy to run the race. As the starting time approached, Judy told Luke, her husband, that the rash was still bothering her. But she ran anyway. Judy had a great start that morning.

Within minutes, Luke was taking pictures with his cell phone, e-mailing photos to family members, and bragging about Judy's pace. Big moments are full of tiny details—some happy, some sad—all seemingly routine and part of performance.

By the end of the race, Judy had slowed to a walk; she was in pain and scared. She complained to Luke of a sore, swollen torso and other problems. When Luke rushed her to a nearby hospital, the doctors said it was likely nothing more than heartburn but, after some concern, they wheeled her to the operating room for exploratory surgery. When the doctors found Luke in the waiting room, their news floored him. "Judy is in a life-and-death struggle to reverse an invasive Strep A infection," they told Luke. They had already removed one dangerously infected organ.

> *Questions to ask yourself as you continue to read Judy's story:*
> - What happens to capability if common problems spread?
> - What type of professional treats every gripe as just routine?
> - Can you afford not to sort out severe problems?
> - Are potential ravages hard to test for and treat?
> - Is there life after late treatment?

Professionals Often Treat Common Gripes Casually

Strep A's dangers are that it is so *common* and potentially *severe*. It is a familiar one-cell organism, easy to miss or underestimate. One in 20 adults carries Strep A during the winter months. More than one-quarter of children carry it on their skin and elsewhere regularly. Its initial symptoms appear familiar and nonthreatening, usually causing only minor throat and skin infections. It catches the immune system and professionals off-guard by disguising itself in 150 different variations. The medical odds in a case like Judy's are that the infection is not serious, but it deserves to be ruled out as harmless because of its potential danger. If it is caught early, penicillin cures it. If it is allowed to continue unchecked, however, Strep A sometimes wreaks a broad and deep attack on vital body functions. In a case such as Judy's, 70 percent of patients die.

As Judy's blood pressure plunged, crucial organs started to shut down. Judy looked enthusiastic and normal when she arrived at the race. Now, she looked black and blue, as though

> You can't afford not to check seemingly small problems that could broadly affect valuable selling time. If people worry and chatter among themselves excessively about distractions, you may lose your chance to boost your revenue.

she'd been in a train wreck. Although she lay unconscious, inside destruction was raging, and doctors were forced to take drastic measures to save her life.

Surgeons sacrificed many of her functions and future capabilities as they treated her aggressively. The next day, Judy required even more aggressive treatment, and two days after that, doctors had to remove one of her hands and a second foot.

Judy's liver and internal systems couldn't process all the toxic infection and medication that had accumulated in her body. This common, invasive organism and late treatment had effectively destroyed a quarter of Judy's body and her capabilities. It became increasingly difficult to see how she could survive, let alone perform in the same way again. The best and brightest had fought for her life against the consequences of late detection.

If only the virus hadn't been dismissed so easily. If only Judy's complaints had been repeated more boldly. If only the combination of severity and spread had been quickly ruled out instead of readily discounted. If only Judy or the technician had insisted on a clean bill of health before Judy raced, her life would be different today. It's hard to understand the wrath of such a seemingly small enemy so commonly harmless. It's no wonder that some orthopedics now test-swab noses before opening up knees in order to make sure everything else is all right.

In sales we must also "rule out" instead of "play the odds." Like medical professionals, we hear daily complaints about many problems or have the urge to express them ourselves. Sales Blazers don't allow the low likelihood of severity to numb their senses, nor do they worry about every problem. They probe discomforts for potential spread and rule out deep, bitter infection.

Life after Turnaround

Finally, Judy's doctors slowed the onslaught. She awoke and said, "Still here." Stuck in bed, Judy's first weeks of recovery were rough, and rehab was painful. The runner and mother faced the harsh realities of the trauma. "My limbs were my life and gave my love," she said. Her kidneys have now caught up and dialysis is no longer necessary. Judy now races in a different category and gives one-armed hugs that warm and soothe. Running has become personal training, and her spirits have lifted.

On the first anniversary of the day she almost died, Judy sat near her client's starting line with her loved ones excited to see the race. What she lost can never be replaced, but she now races with wheelchairs, cheers for clients, and cares more deeply for family. While her capabilities have changed, Judy's love and ability to race have been restored in a different way through hard work, patience, and incredible creativity.

In sales, a problem that seems severe among the team and is caught late can spread by word of mouth, even after an apparent solution. After damage to selling, livelihoods, or the organization has been stopped, everyone still needs to work to help cure lingering bitterness and distraction.

There are inspiring endings to be had by Sales Blazers, as we shall see, but we need to start with a clean bill of health.

> *Parallels between Judy's Story and Strategy 1*
> - Common problems spread, disabling talent broadly.
> - Salespeople are leaders and must guard against treating gripes as just routine.
> - You can't afford not to identify and treat severe distractions.
> - Hidden, potential ravages aren't hard to test for and treat.
> - Even if you're the problem, there is life after treatment.

THE SOLUTION: START WITH A CLEAN BILL OF HEALTH

Judy's story illustrates the two steps to gaining a clean bill of health: (1) detect early any potentially *severe* problems, and (2) quickly treat *common* problems that could spread. It's the same in the world of revenue growth. Starting with a clean bill of health can prevent key difficulties from hampering prospects' and salespeople's ability to focus on critical tasks and success. It means dealing with hard-to-find, hard-to-take truths before leading in a new direction.

One vice president at a well-known company asked, "Are the small things really that destructive? They're not going to kill the company." Maybe it isn't a big problem that a single salesperson does some of the clerical work that someone else has been hired to do, but if the practice starts to spread throughout the force and clients see less of our face or hear less of our voice, then revenue will stall. Even if we can replace the revenue, we can never replace the time, and time is the second variable of growth.

Also, some problems that may not seem serious to a manager or executives are critical to frontline reps. One group I worked with helped illustrate this. Leadership received what seemed to be a small, occasional complaint—an unusual failure in a health-care benefit that didn't cover a particular medical procedure. No big deal, right? But the people affected started complaining to each other.

For most people the lack of coverage wasn't much of an issue and was worth only an occasional comment. However, a group of salespeople with young children was hit hard. Some were facing up to $25,000 in family expense. Management didn't pay attention to the problem because the plan was traditional and was considered equitable for the entire workforce. However, the people affected were often focused on a solution to a $25,000 medical expense instead of on the next sale. Problems that don't affect managers often seem benign and remain hidden. From the salesperson's vantage point, they are critical.

Seeing Hidden Problems

To understand why successful leaders call some problems "hidden," it helps to understand that we all have a blind spot. Many of our actions have well-understood and intended effects on the people we try to lead. At other times, our efforts and policies result in unintended, painful consequences that others must deal with because we don't see them. For example, long-time observation of businesspeople has shown that all managers have blind spots regarding how their policies and actions affect others.

Two of the reasons a leader rises in station are confidence and experience, but these strengths can also create blind spots. Years of experience give leaders confidence in their ability to determine whether a complaint is really a problem. That confidence sometimes slips into overconfidence about how their actions are affecting people they are trying to lead. An issue comes up and, because they've seen it so many times, they dismiss it without giving it their full attention.

Problems also hide in blind spots because usually people criticize a leader's weaknesses only among themselves. Sometimes hard workers presume leadership's indifference and don't say anything. There are times when it may be career-limiting for even the boldest people to broach the subject of a manager's weakness, however tactfully. These workers may remain outwardly silent but begin to chatter with others behind the scenes. The analogy is Judy thinking her infection wasn't important enough to keep mentioning, given everything else that was going on around her. While she didn't persist with the professionals, she did tell her husband, though he could do very little about it.

For people in the business of producing revenue, chatter infects motivation deeply and spreads broadly, hampering sales. Does this mean we should try to find every problem and treat it? No. It is critical that complaints be judged quickly case by case for the severity of their impact on selling and for their potential to spread. Life and business are full of resistance; it is only the severe dangers to our goals that we are trying to isolate and clear.

Overreacting to Judy's infection could have killed her just as easily as the Strep A itself. A fearful person who tries to fix every problem won't cause revenue growth. However, it's also dangerous for a professional leader to try to motivate without examining and ruling out a problem's impact on selling and potential to spread.

By itself action on severe distractions doesn't guarantee maximum sales, any more than getting a clean bill of health replaces physical exertion. Cleaning up severe, negative factors simply makes it possible for leaders to do the positive work that will be necessary.

The pivotal position of a Sales Blazer relies on the leverage of contact with all the team members (see Figure 1.1). Sales Blazers are also the force that removes hindrances to performance to raise results.

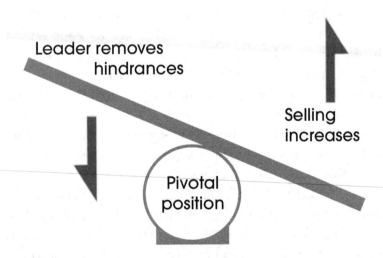

Figure 1.1 Leadership and Motivational Hygiene

Psychologist, author, and business guru Frederick Herzberg perhaps best explained the difference between cleaning up negative problems and creating positive change. Herzberg showed that positive management moves that "satisfy" differ from "removing dissatisfaction" and that both are needed to increase productivity. Herzberg's Motivation Hygiene Theory labeled the positive acts of leaders that enhance job satisfaction as motivators and problems that lead to dissatisfaction as hygiene factors. Hygiene factors hamper motivation and prevent improving results.

DETECTING WEAKNESS

So where should a leader begin looking for weaknesses that could potentially ravage results? Sales force capabilities. In every budget cycle, sales and company leadership come together and invest a staggering amount of resources to deploy a sales force. These complex sales forces rely on four major areas of expertise that should be familiar: people policies, sales force deployment, information management, and leadership. These areas of expertise can be broken down into 21 more specific capabilities (see Figure 1.2). Unlike divisions that depend on others for these capabilities, sales often relies on salespeople to at least partially own them. They are the moving parts that make the force healthy—or not.

All of the capabilities shown in Figure 1.2 can quietly go south without leadership even knowing. Sales Blazers don't

Figure 1.2 Sales Force Capabilities

start by becoming the best at each capability; they start by finding and treating the extreme problems with these capabilities. If a sales team widely rates even a couple of the 21 capabilities as worse than problematic—for example, "severely dysfunctional: completely inhibits focus on selling"—revenue growth may not happen. If several are spreading ravage, it won't matter how right management is on an issue or what (unrelated) positive steps they took. The confidence to be open enough to look for and find flaws in the status quo is a needed strength, not a weakness.

The 21 capabilities are where you want to start looking. There may be areas that you may not completely control.

Other areas may seem too routine to require constant attention. When something that should support selling quietly turns against it, a Sales Blazer recognizes it. As one leader said, "In all honesty, there are always things getting in the way of selling. How you identify, acknowledge, and pursue a quick resolution is key to long-term success."

Examples of Detection in the Field

The following are a few brief observations of problems that may seem small but were actually hampering capabilities (numbered as in Figure 1.2).

A negative view that one CEO regularly *communicated (17)* about the sales force had salespeople and leaders looking for a new job. One VP of sales explained, "I remember the first time the CEO spoke. He stood up and said things that made salespeople question their future with the company. In some companies, the sales force is treated as the reason we all have jobs and can continue our mission. But our new CEO kept speaking as though the force were a necessary evil. The word spread instantly through the field, killing motivation and starting an exodus. Instead of leading, the CEO *communicated* how he really felt—that the sales force was a pain in the neck."

This message broadly sabotaged hope—the lifeblood of revenue producers. Ask yourself: "Would anyone volunteer to tell this CEO about the effect on selling that his communication problem had?" A Sales Blazer would courageously offer the CEO feedback about the effect his comments were having on sales.

An example of dysfunctional *teamwork (21)* that I observed occurred when one rep made a sport of "blasting" the members of a second sales team to the support personnel. The second team's manager or members had no idea what was being said about them. What might have seemed like harmless competition was actually causing support to procrastinate on callbacks to the seemingly unreasonable sales team. A Sales Blazer detects *teamwork* issues by maintaining an open dialogue with individuals and other departments.

A great example of multiple issues came from Joan and Jane, two telecom salespeople in New York. What they told me was a clear reminder that occasionally, as sales leaders, we get so busy that we lose sight of the damaging misperceptions we create—misperceptions that could be easily cleared up with detection.

"After six months, our manager still locks himself in his office," Jane explained. "He comes out twice a day to bark orders or ask about some client." That's an unhealthy way to gain pipeline *progress (20)*.

They spoke also of the manager's questionable *coaching (16)* tactics.

"He never helps," Jane continued. "He sometimes even hurls personal insults in front of everyone. Then, he goes back in as usual and shuts his door and does who knows what until he sneaks out. We don't see or hear from him for days.

"He talks *goals (15)* but ignores us every time we ask if we can renew goals since we had a personal leave. . . . He just brushes it off and says, 'Quit whining about it.' Oh, if that jerk only knew."

The sting of these perceptions was painful to hear and obviously one-sided. You might assume that these two sales reps are near the bottom of the rankings, but they aren't. Joan is near the top and Jane is near the middle. When they were asked if they'd shared their viewpoint with the manager, Joan replied, "Yeah, right. So we can lose our jobs before we find new ones?"

Joan and Jane were, however, open about keeping each other up-to-date on their job hunting—certainly not the results a team working on a promising *retention (5)* strategy wants.

"The dumb thing is that I like what I do," said Joan. "If he'd just fix a couple of things, I'd stop looking and stay. I'd put up with all the other annoying things and just do my job." Imagine how difficult it will be for this manager to launch some new leadership initiative before he has detected and treated some of these harsh misperceptions. Just by opening up *communication (17)*, he'd likely detect a majority of the gripes and be able to treat the severe pain. As I listened, I thought, "At best, these issues are eating up 10 percent of the salespeople's efforts, effectively hindering them from blazing ahead to new growth. At worst, these perceptions will progress until they unnecessarily turn terminal for all three jobs."

Maybe the most dangerous enemies of selling time sneak in from the salesperson's side—meaning the rep is hurting his or her own productivity without being aware of it or perhaps even being in denial. As a salesperson considers sales force deployment issues, he or she must consider *self-deployment*—how time is spent. In other words, what are recent examples of how I've covered the territory or assignment inefficiently? In which instances has my own disorganization eaten away at selling time? Have I made efforts outside of work time to build a needed capability? Have I mastered the company's suggested sales process, including time management practices? Have I done so for days, weeks, and months before doing things in the way that I think they should be done? Have I utilized marketing and support capabilities and teamed with related personnel effectively?

I found that the extra hours people spend every week distracted by serious issues or complaining about potentially contagious issues with peers doesn't just come out of personal time. The distractions' effects occur before, during, and after critical selling moments.

Some threats to getting the job done don't stem from internal company imperfections or personal inefficiencies but from new competitor activity or from politics within client organizations. We discuss getting around delays with clients and competing reps in the chapters that follow, but once an internal or personal danger to selling is detected, what do Sales Blazers do to treat severe, spreading distractions? Let's take a look at some examples.

Examples of Treatment in the Field

One Sales Blazer in the financial sector, who was fairly new in his position and facing a steep sales objective, recapped dozens of observations about improving goal setting. Previous goal setting for bonuses had killed motivation in several territories because marketing hadn't discontinued confusing advertising in those territories. If this leader hadn't gone looking, he probably would have interpreted the situation as merely a problem of poor talent.

"We all want to think we get everything right—it's our job," he said. "The problem is we're not all-knowing. I can't know what every unintentional ramification is in the field of the decisions I make. I know the important effect: revenue growth. I know salespeople will always think goals are too high. But when you don't hear one single complaint about a major change in some new program, it's time to go looking."

After hearing only silence instead of the usual complaints about a large increase he had made in bonus *goals*, this leader asked us to administer an anonymous assessment—a sales bill of health—to members at every level of the team. This made it safe for salespeople to tell him he'd just turned what were stretch goals into completely irrelevant numbers for smaller markets with confusing advertising. He didn't even come close to implementing every idea of reps in the affected areas, but because of what he heard broadly, he did decide to lower select goals for bonuses and to look into the advertising problem. Without making the effort to detect something he might not know about, he wouldn't have seen what was killing motivation or demand until it was too late to affect period sales.

Scores of other Sales Blazers treated communication breakdowns just by listening to other people's perspectives. The tone of appreciation of those who work with Sales Blazers can't be captured in words, but read the comments from coworkers and decide if your teammates would say these things about you.

Sales Blazers' teammates said that they "respond to teammates and truly listen to what they have to say," and that these salespeople behave like respected leaders who carefully offer "feedback" and "unending support." Those who lead teams show "support and advocacy of the team to higher ups." Sales Blazers in general "listen to other perspectives and ideas without immediately discounting them" while "being totally honest, open, and transparent. We really want to work hard with them."

Comments by people working with Sales Blazers made it clear that these leaders replaced shortsightedness with advocacy. They have an ability to "ask questions, listen, and then take action," then "make decisions based on facts." They show an unrelenting "adaptability to change." As one salesperson said, "Growth leaders gain a clear definition of the problem through gathering facts and knowledge. Then they work with the team and follow up." One Sales Blazer was said to have "persistence in follow-through and advocacy with issues. He's always working with other senior management members to facilitate and implement needed change."

Note the affect on their team that others attributed to Sales Blazers. They said their team has a "high level of communication between lower and executive management to keep the channels open and clear with no gray areas." This type of effort will help you build the awareness and trust that allow people to open up and aid diagnosis and treatment, because they "know the leader is working hard to support us."

A coworker made this point about Kari, a Sales Blazer at Harbour Air Seaplanes. Kari "takes note of what others say about issues at group meetings and even at events like fun nights. She has the ability to utilize the intelligence of the team by listening to them, valuing their opinions, and applying some of their better suggestions. Kari's willingness to ask, listen, solve problems, and utilize suggestions is key to growth."

Listening, looking, and inviting input about the most serious issues hampering growth—as well as listening to solutions and taking on the challenge of relieving hindrances—is common among Sales Blazers.

THE DIFFERENCE

To identify serious weaknesses, one needs just enough humility to be self-critical and "get things out of the way of selling." Sales Blazers quickly determine which problems to treat by sensing the severity and spread from the vantage point of both the employee and the company.

Bo, whom we met in the Introduction, described what this strategy looks like. "I was relentless in protecting my people from distractions," Bo explained. "Administrative stuff, unrelated training stuff, anything that wasn't critical, problems that had no place on a team with a challenge like this ahead of us. I looked for anything I needed to get out of the way.

"It really took a lot of one-on-one time with each individual to stay on top of distractions and to help each person understand that there was a way for the plan to work. I said, 'Granted it's a long-shot, granted there are some things that don't look likely, granted there are some challenges across the board. But if I can remove most of these and create a sequence of events for you that helps you see that it's not physically impossible, will you trust me enough to say that you'll work with us with your head in the game?'"

Revenue Boost

By listening before taking action, as Bo did, Sales Blazers gain a clean bill of health. But does getting a clean bill of health create real growth? Yes. Michael Greenbaum, like most growth-company CEOs, leads the sales charge at his company, CyraCom. He led his company to be featured in *INC.* as one of the 500 fastest-growing companies in the United States. How? His people told me, "Michael is a master at paying attention to large and small issues and removing key problems before they affect performance. He's excellent at facilitating through challenges by quickly getting to a solution right there and then, so those affected can move on to revenue-related activity. This is a key reason our growth rate has averaged nearly 40 percent annually. We have sustained this for three years."

Clearing things up worked for others, too. Steve, a Sales Blazer at a call center, began by listening and solving the most severe problems. The result? Call center revenue was going nowhere before he improved it more than 100 percent.

While Lou's emergency transportation counterparts were struggling for any growth in a highly bureaucratic industry, Lou led his Western team at American Medical Response (AMR) to year-over-year growth and number 1 in the company. Lou's people say, "He's not just our leader. He's like a snowplow that clears everything out of our way so we can perform."

Gary of Pfizer is a team player who listens and then "leads by example" to heal complaints. Gary's team sharpened their focus by improving morale, and productivity increased. How? The team focused on overcoming a few critical obstacles, which opened up new ways to develop sales never before apparent. Gary's team increased their sales performance from near last in the area (47 out of 53) to first in their region and on top of their area in a short 12 months. Probing, listening, and responding works.

> *A better approach:* Mediocre salespeople are oblivious to small but extreme problems and overconfident about what they think is going on in the team. Sales Blazers know they must be self-critical and assess perceptions objectively to find and clear up severe distractions before they affect performance.

Starting with a clean bill of health does not mean that if, for example, you see a spill on the floor at the store, you recommend a "remodel on aisle five"; rather, it means to take a moment and direct the more appropriate "cleanup on aisle five" for a spilled item that could be dangerous. Great performers commit to open but accurate communications with their clients and leaders; great leaders do the same with their teams. Accept a little inconvenience and get that checkup before diving into a rigorous sales plan. Remember Judy's story as we embark on more positive strides to extraordinary growth in the chapters that follow. Without overreacting, absolutely gain awareness and treat the most severe dangers to productivity and goals before beginning the quarter.

Figure 1.3 is a sample Sales Bill of Health that makes it safe to rate potentially painful issues anonymously and help you or the salespeople around you to consider objectively any personal or client issues that are ravaging selling time (also see www.salesblazers.com). The items listed in the Sales Bill of Health are meant to be broad nets to catch any severe problem and gain a baseline for vital statistics that affect future chapters. It's not critical what my definitions of these items are; it's more important to let the people you query interpret each item however they like or to rephrase the item so it applies specifically to your company or situation. After, we'll explore how to treat the results.

WHAT TO DO WITH THE RESULTS OF A SALES BILL OF HEALTH

During my years of research, I repeatedly heard from sales and support people how relieved they were when someone in a position to help asked about something that was endangering their revenue growth and then fixed the problem. Checking your people anonymously for extreme issues hindering the

Sales Bill of Health

Please rate each item's impact on your selling and results.

Sales Force Capabilities	4 Greatly Enhances My Selling	3 Moderately Enhances My Selling	2 Moderately Distracts My Selling	1 Severely Hinders My Selling
1. Hiring	O	O	O	O
2. Compensation	O	O	O	O
3. Benefits	O	O	O	O
4. Training	O	O	O	O
5. Rep Retention/Workplace	O	O	O	O
6. Territory/Accts.	O	O	O	O
7. Organization Structure	O	O	O	O
8. Team Competencies	O	O	O	O
9. Sales Process	O	O	O	O
10. Marketing/Support	O	O	O	O
11. Target/Market Info.	O	O	O	O
12. Financial Analysis	O	O	O	O
13. Admin. Processes	O	O	O	O
14. Info./Tech. Tools	O	O	O	O
15. Goal Setting	O	O	O	O
16. Coaching	O	O	O	O
17. Communication	O	O	O	O
18. Awards & Recognition	O	O	O	O
19. Facilitation	O	O	O	O
20. Personal Progress/Career	O	O	O	O
21. Teamwork	O	O	O	O

YOUR Effectiveness

22. Client & Prospect Coverage	O	O	O	O
23. Organization/Time Mgt.	O	O	O	O
24. Key Competencies	O	O	O	O
25. Use of Selling Process	O	O	O	O
26. Accessing Support	O	O	O	O

CLIENTS' Potential Obstacles

27. Access to Client Executives	O	O	O	O
28. Features/Solution Fit	O	O	O	O
29. Decision Made Elsewhere	O	O	O	O
30. Purchase Process	O	O	O	O
31. Timing Delays	O	O	O	O
32. Unavailable Information	O	O	O	O

Figure 1.3 Sales Bill of Health

Sales Bill of Health (Continued)

Please mark the most accurate response to each statement.

Activities of Influence	4 Always	3 Usually	2 Sometimes	1 Never
33. I know my contacts':				
-current job goals	O	O	O	O
-career goals	O	O	O	O
-personal goals	O	O	O	O
34. I know my contacts' efforts to directly impact executives' goals.	O	O	O	O
35. I get specialists to help in my selling efforts.	O	O	O	O
36. I receive weekly coaching.	O	O	O	O
37. I coach someone each week.	O	O	O	O
38. I receive feedback weekly.	O	O	O	O
39. I offer feedback weekly.	O	O	O	O
40. I celebrate others' success daily.	O	O	O	O
41. I reward others' success uniquely.	O	O	O	O
42. My success is recognized weekly.	O	O	O	O

Key Selling Activity   Please Answer Below.

43. Of all the activities required to make a sale the one which has the most impact is:

_____

  • The most important thing to do during this step is:_____

_____

  • I know I have completed the step successfully when:_____

_____

  • I spend _____ hours each week actively engaged in this step.

44. I speak (not including e-mail) to unsold prospects _____ hours each week.

45. I speak (not including e-mail) to current clients _____ hours each week.

46. The client need that overlaps most with his or her leadership's urgencies is:

_____

sales force may rehash predictable gripes, but it's important to do. We now have a tool to uncover our blind spot—a Sales Bill of Health. The successful leaders I observed seemed to have a mantra: "Revenue is the goal, not fulfilling my ego. Leadership means drawing out and tackling even tough issues first."

We have already covered some examples of capabilities that can become dysfunctional. It is easy to have salespeople rate the internal capabilities, personal work distractions, and potential client issues, and even provide open-ended comments. I'd love to tell you what you'll find, but that's the point of asking— none of us knows yet. Every organization and every set of people is different, but you can detect severe problems and decide whether to treat them or just listen.

How should you react to results? At this point, we are only looking to detect and treat problems that are rated "Severely hindering my selling." Asking about all capabilities and issues at once forces a comparative response. So, which distractions should you treat? Those that you can actually control and that are widely rated "severely hindering my selling." These are likely dysfunctional. Should you then go on to items with average ratings? No. Trying to make the world perfect instead of selling is like trying to set statistical records on your bill of health before beginning your training for a marathon—we're just trying to pass so we can get moving. Focusing on normal problems is a danger to selling in and of itself. The answer is to check for severe dangers to selling and then get going.

Remember, treating negatives is an entirely separate effort from creating positives. We will make critical positive moves in the chapters that follow, but detecting the most disruptive issues is the way to start with a clean bill of health.

FINAL, IMPORTANT THOUGHTS

Those responsible for revenue have little time for engaging in or listening to moaning. Leadership opportunities that I have experienced have convinced me that there isn't much time in the upbeat world of revenue for discussing cynical topics with habitual complainers. However, whatever you call them—complaints, distractions, issues, problems, weaknesses, or hygiene issues—you must fix those that are severely hampering selling time.

I asked Jon, who sells health-care data systems for GE, if starting with a clean bill of health is really important. "It is incredibly important to check once in a while to see if something you or the company is doing is getting in the way of sales," he told me. "Motivators who failed me in past lives are those who ignorantly refused to see or do anything about a glaring problem, and just told you to get selling. The leaders who succeeded were those who actively tried to get things out of my way that didn't need to be there."

Jon told me that many times the most important thing you can do to progress a sale is to ask yourself what is in the way and then move it.

Even if you discover something serious, it's much better to face it now. After treatment, life is good and the career continues. For example, the joy that Judy feels training clients and watching them smile after a race is real. The joy from raising her child is real—these are measures of true success.

In driving sales, too, you may have to treat some things to start to gain a clean bill of health. You'll be glad you did, because you'll witness the emotional release of those you lead. You will see the distractions dissipate and focus on the process return. You'll also open up a healthy, honest dialogue. This will make it possible to do what we'll do next—find out what makes people tick and the most effective ways to motivate them.

Strategy Summary—Start with a Clean Bill of Health

1. Show the courage to identify and remove the most serious, potentially common problems hampering results. Embrace the contradiction between confidence and the discipline to be self-critical. It is part of the job for a Sales Blazer.

2. Don't just appease, and do not try to fix every problem that arises or attempt to create unparalleled strengths out of severe problems. Remain focused on quickly healing, not perfecting, normal problems, then move on to action.

3. Separate problems that are normal from those that severely threaten your selling. Sales Blazers have the discipline to listen for silence and to detect problems within topics that are impossible for clients or reps to share.

4. Clearing up a seemingly small issue that has been distracting someone from progressing toward results is liberating and revenue-producing.

Spark a Performance Pursuit

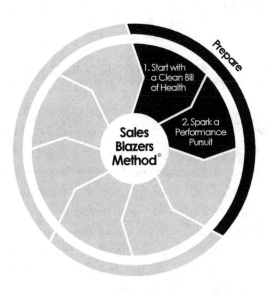

THE STRATEGY

Learn the most passionate ambitions of the people you need to influence. Turn their tasks into opportunities to pursue career and personal achievement. Commit, as a leader, to making other people's pursuits a priority—*Spark a Performance Pursuit*.

What we will accomplish in this chapter: We will explore the growing disconnect between firms and salespeople. We will discover what the most powerful motivations are and strengthen their ties to selling. We will spark a relentless pursuit within everyone responsible for revenue.

THE PROBLEM: A GROWING DIVIDE BETWEEN COMPANY AND SALESPERSON

Some people in sales focus completely on quotas, closes, and commissions—for them, that's all there is. Trying to be "all business," they may lose touch with how people are influenced by larger personal and economic drivers. They haven't awakened to the facts that (1) companies are increasingly less loyal over the long term, (2) today's performers are less loyal, and (3) great leaders bridge this divide in innovative ways.

To spark a performance pursuit does not require that you add even more hours to your already overloaded schedule. Instead, it replaces trivial conversations en route, at lunch, or during one-on-one meetings with meaningful, enlightening inquiries into the other person's ambitions.

Tim, one of my sales mentors, advised, "Trust is key as you try to motivate; in the sense that whomever you are trying to motivate must trust that you are really worthy of trust—trustworthy—because you have their best interest at heart."

Tim pointed out that sincere interest in those you lead promotes loyalty between you and them as you champion their personal success. If you don't know what moves those you are trying to lead, you won't be able to motivate improved performance.

"But if you don't commit to earn trust, the whole thing will backfire on you," Tim cautioned.

Companies Are Less Loyal

In sales, it is not just about having a nice place to work; it's also about long-term prosperity and developing unique capabilities. For example, salespeople experience an obvious, though often denied, decrease in corporate loyalty every day. They see friends' frozen pensions, tentative career paths, reduced benefits, reorganizations, and more. Some companies have "right-sized" and pressured their people beyond healthy limits. This has created a virtual workforce of "free agents," left to endure a risky future alone.

Even if your company isn't slashing benefits that help build long-term prosperity for employees, you probably see it happening to friends and family, and you know the tide of corporate benefits is going out. Ironically, some executives push a company vision and career path they know half the rank-and-file won't be around to follow. At any given moment, 54 percent of today's workers have five or fewer years left at their company. This is due partly to differences in thinking and new positions made available by retiring baby boomers, and the positions that salespeople vacate are the most difficult to replace.

Employees Are Less Loyal

It's not just companies that are behaving in disloyal ways; salespeople have become more fickle, too. With the wealth of new opportunities available, workers are becoming more mobile, and workforces are shifting. Fifty percent of employees spend part of their day actively looking for new work. Even companies that had low turnover previously are susceptible. The result? Instead of selling, salespeople spend time mapping personal detours they find necessary for future career, personal, and financial success. The next paycheck isn't the only motive people have; future pay and career progress are key.

There is no longer a standard workforce with a singular loyalty. Cultures and markets increasingly overlap. The global workforce is mixing and diversifying teams. Workers are entering the field increasingly younger and less experienced; they stay in the workforce longer, but they switch jobs more frequently. Generational sprawl and new diversity mean the life philosophies and goals of performers and management don't always match up.

More diverse teams, sensing less company loyalty, expect more autonomy and influence than ever before. They look to make work more rewarding within a career, not just lucrative this quarter. Companies that want talent to stay need to help salespeople find "balance" and "opportunities for personal growth."

A House with Two Homes

The work that salespeople do to build future capabilities translates into dollars. They spend so much time at work that it becomes a home away from home. When firms turn their backs on committing to salespeople's future security, the relationship changes—each is suddenly chasing very different goals. It's like a separation taking place in a home with a divorce around the corner—the residents are still sharing a house, but with separate entrances and pursuing separate goals.

There is a clear, emerging disconnect between what leaders believe employees want and what employees actually consider important. For example, employees rank personal "growth" and "earnings potential" second only to "compensation" and "benefits"—a focus on "my" future needs. A great place to work is just a prerequisite.

Some companies understand the value of talent, but even these companies can drop the ball when it comes to providing salespeople with the future needs they seek.

It may not be possible to fire up pensions and long-term career paths, but companies must find ways to build longer-term relationships with salespeople. In the future, management innovations that do this are going to be critical to a company's gaining productivity. Sales Blazers learn how to harness and leverage the new knowledge and innovation-creating employee that is emerging. Leaders are in a unique position to repair the relationship and benefit financially.

THE SOLUTION: SPARK A PERFORMANCE PURSUIT

Commissions and job security are only the basics. Salespeople are going to chase what they need on all levels. Salespeople's full focus will have to be earned with a new type of investment—a whole new source of unifying engagement. Sales Blazers make the job align with what individuals need on all levels, instead of just trying to align others to company goals and money. Great leaders embrace personal visions and career plans as new sources of motivation. This isn't just being nice. Often people who need to lead others focus on being "one of the guys" rather than on really understanding what drives those around them and helping everyone pull in a uniquely meaningful way but together in the same direction.

Could you gain more ground faster with a horse headed home or a horse headed up the mountain? To describe what the strategy of *Spark a Performance Pursuit* is all about, a story comes to mind—a brush with massive strength and determination.

Chaquita's Home

On the first day of my most recent sales management role, Mark Ludwig told me, "You are going to love this job because we have all the thoroughbreds in place. They are amazing. All we do is lead this power."

His reference to thoroughbreds illustrated immediately what kind of potential strength and direction he was talking about. He wasn't saying that people are horses, but his remark made me think of my first ride on Chaquita.

When I was a boy, I visited Thousand Peaks Ranch, which was owned by a family friend. It is no ordinary ranch. Thousand Peaks encompasses an entire beautiful valley, high in the Rockies, surrounded by mountainous spires.

That first day, we decided to go horseback riding. I rode Chaquita. We took the horses up through the forest and beyond the river for a long ride. Chaquita was a gorgeous, obedient horse, and I could feel her pick up as I prodded her along. Occasionally, she'd get distracted and slow down to graze, but a gentle tug at the reins was all it took to get her on the path again. We finally reached the summit, where we stopped for a breathtaking view of snow-capped mountains. I'll never forget what happened next.

As I pulled the reins toward home, my legs felt an explosive series of tremors from the horse. The massive change in momentum was instantly terrifying, and the direction certain and unstoppable. In the following moments, we covered more ground than we had in an hour on the way up. I was helpless to stop this powerful animal; all I could do was dodge the branches.

Chaquita was going home, and there was no stopping her.

My role changed from director to passenger in the instant the ride became a pursuit. All horses are different, but a well-treated horse on a large ranch loves to go home. Home is where there's food, security, the herd, pecking order, freedom, and play—*everything important.*

> *A horse's perspective of home:* Home offers food, security, the herd, pecking order, freedom, and play—everything important to a horse.

That day I learned that, for Chaquita, her own motivation was a more powerful and permanent source of incentive than reins and spurs. Even an apple didn't compare to everything important to this horse. For Chaquita, the powerful change in effort and direction was what I now call sparking a performance pursuit. This powerful change in effort and direction, if charted, would look like a spike in sales. By the same token, Sales Blazers gain top performance by finding a way to employ "horses headed home." The most talented salespeople, like horses, don't mind hard work; they just want to pursue what is most important to them.

All Horses Are Different

Salespeople are human; they aren't horses. However, as Ludwig noted, there are powerful lessons in their similar explosive tendencies. To learn more about directing this power of momentum, I decided to consult with experts. Consider what Terry, a horse trainer from Churchill Downs, said.

"Chaquita behaved typically for a ranch or farm horse," Terry explained. "But all horses don't run to the ranch. Horses we have here are racehorses, and they go from track to track to track. They have no home—home is freedom. A lot of these horses may be out of their stalls only an hour a day. When they're loose, they're just happy to be free. It really all begins with each horse. Every horse is different."

Terry explained that you can't inspire all thoroughbreds the same way; each has unique motivations. "Some of them just naturally want to run, some of them are a little lazy, and some you have to really get after to get them to go," he said. "You've got good ones that don't bite, you've got biters, and you've got horses that are just plain mean."

I asked how he gets the truly mean horses to perform.

"Don't start out assuming they're mean," he said. "You have to get to know them. They may just be careful and will finally let you in. Some horses prefer being left alone. You can only do so much." Terry explained that if you can't reach a truly mean horse, even by leaving it alone, your time might be better spent on another horse.

As I listened to Terry, I wondered, "If horses are sparked in different ways, how does this idea expand the metaphor?" Then Terry explained that he focuses on treating the individual horse uniquely, and using what each likes to do to get him or her to respond and perform.

"They're all different. You just find what each individual horse likes to do and work with it."

Like horses, some people are born to sell, while some must be trained or refocused, but most will respond to this type of individual motivation.

"Take Prima Serita," Terry said. "Prima Serita is a really sweet, kind horse. She gets treated a lot differently than the others. She loves life and people. She doesn't try to hurt you. I love that horse and she performs for us. But I've got horses over there that will try to hurt you. Those I don't play with as much as I do Prima Serita. She's just a lot nicer to be around."

Terry explained that Prima Serita responds to individual attention by performing better—a lot better. But she's also a thoroughbred, and like all thoroughbreds, she's bred to run. That's what she knows.

Wanting to connect the performance with the treatment, I asked, "Does Prima Serita run faster because of your treatment?"

"She runs beautifully," Terry replied. "She loves to run for us."

Sensing a truth about evaluating new salespeople, I asked, "Did you always know she would?"

"Very early," he answered. "When horses are first starting out, there are things you look for. One is how well they work in the morning. Every once in a while, you'll get a horse that we call a 'morning glory,' one that works hard in the morning but won't run in the afternoon or in races. It's hard to get these horses to win. Generally, you go by the way they work. You've got to know and work with each one closely to see what each one really has in them. It's great to get a horse that goes out and gets the fast times."

Debbie Foley, an experienced trainer of show horses and president of Silver Brooks Stables, added another perspective about my experience riding Chaquita home.

"In some aspects," she said, "horses are like people. There are some who need to be motivated and some who are self-motivated." As far as Chaquita wanting to go home, she explained, "It's true that barrel racers refer to the last leg as 'going home,' and the horse may take off on that leg faster than any other. On the other hand, our horses are show horses, and each one is unique. Some run, some won't."

Home Is Where the Heart Is—Inside

Loren, the owner of Thousand Peaks Ranch, tied it all together when I called him recently. Loren remembered my own white-knuckle ride on Chaquita so many years ago and said, "You have to remember that home is where the heart is, even for a horse. Nine times out of ten, a horse will always take off for home, wherever that is, because it is where it wants to be and it has everything the horse needs most."

I asked Loren how the "bred-to-run" behavior of thoroughbreds relates to the other horses.

"When a horse loves to run, and most do, and they start to run toward home, riders get an exciting ride just like you got. It's not as much the home outside as the home *inside* that makes them who they are and makes all horses the same. They'll all run through whatever they need to run through in order to get home, whatever that means to them. Our horses love to run toward home because the ranch is such a great place for them."

Blazing to get to "the home inside"—this resonated with observations of how Sales Blazers motivate themselves and others.

The few horses that won't run for any reason are the exception and might need to be replaced. As the horse masters said, "Point the horse home." A load is hardly a concern for the horse when the horse's power is aroused. It's what sparks a performance pursuit.

> *Blazer horse sense:* Great sales leaders discover the most passionate pursuits of each person—what they were born to be—and find a way to make that part of the work.

It may be tempting to see this strategy as giving in to whatever the salesperson wants. Not so. The task you ask of other people feels lighter and is carried out best if they're also pursuing what's most important to them.

Sales Blazers pull away from the masses by understanding how to lead people whose hopes are only assisted by money.

At Horizon Business Systems, Bill's team has been "selling printed communication products with double-digit growth for 15 years in a declining niche." His people said that Bill is a perfect example of leading humans, not numbers, to success. The sales team knows Bill will do whatever it takes to help them. They characterize him as a "true friend and cheerleader." He encourages staff to "grow beyond current boundaries."

One of Bill's six-figure salespeople observed that among Bill's strengths is his ability to "create a culture consistent with what I value" and "to understand and assist me in my personal goals for success in life."

Sales Blazers champion people's success in very individual ways, knowing that a rapid change in sales results will follow. This does not mean they get distracted helping performers chase goals that are unrelated to work. Rather, Sales Blazers creatively find overlap in goals—the home inside—and make them part of the job.

THE WAY TO A SALESPERSON'S HEART

How do you spark a performance pursuit in someone you're leading and get a change in momentum similar to what I got from Chaquita? First, you have to know what each person is really after—remember, your competitors offer pay and commissions, too. Second, you have to know how to weave work goals with a person's passionate pursuits.

First, how do you find out a person's most profound passions? Famous behavioral scientist Abraham Maslow gave us a place to start. Adding practical detail to Maslow's Hierarchy of Needs, as shown in Figure 2.1, lets you use it as a tool to get specific about a person's motivations—the home inside.

Connecting each layer of the graphic in Figure 2.1 to a person's real-life experiences gives a leader powerful insight. Start with the basics of the Physical layer at the bottom. For example, one of the people you lead may have a need for a new house or major repair, and this is one of the biggest physical needs on his or her mind. On an even more basic level, do you know your people's and their spouses' favorite foods?

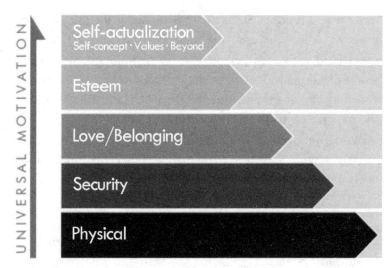

Figure 2.1 Maslow's Hierarchy of Needs

How about Security? Have you ever asked how your people were treated at previous jobs? Do you really understand the reasons they left? Do you think similar issues might ever affect how they work now?

Once commissions and the job are secure, sales and support people continue to build relationships, seeking to Belong and seeking Esteem from others. These needs include families and any other groups to which they belong, but they also have to do with how individuals feel about where they fall within the pecking order among their colleagues. Have you glimpsed their expectations for recognition? Become aware.

The highest need, Self-actualization, includes the most profound pursuits of any human. A salesperson passionately pursues higher aspirations, what he or she values most, to achieve major goals, to practice altruism, and to define himself or herself in a better way. Maslow's Self-actualization needs include becoming more of who you are—reaching beyond yourself. Do you understand who each person you try to influence was born to be—professionally and personally? Even seasoned performers who may act as though they've "arrived" are usually still passionately trying to get somewhere.

By learning about the aspirations your people think about every day, you can discover their most powerful and persistent motivations—the home inside.

> *Find out your people's aspirations and weave them into job goals.* To accelerate assignments related to your sales by using a person's passions requires awareness, understanding, and respect for the person's pursuits. This should be more than marching through Maslow; it should become a natural conversation. We're not talking about changing company goals for individuals; we're talking about changing how individuals see company goals.

THE CHICHEN ITZA CHAT

For years, performance experts have been building a foundation on Maslow's hierarchy without really applying it effectively to the sales job; let's see how adding something I call a *Chichen Itza Chat* can help you do this realistically.

If you've ever visited the ruins at Chichen Itza on the Yucatan Peninsula in Mexico, you know that the Mayan pyramids there have steps, unlike the pyramids in Egypt. You can walk up each side. The main pyramid, however, has only three scalable sides that have been restored; the fourth is crumbling and dangerous (see Figure 2.2).

Maslow's hierarchy applies to a salesperson's work much better if four dimensions, or sides, are added so that it becomes a pyramid. The sides capture the four aspects of a salesperson's life: (1) intimate, (2) personal, (3) career, and (4) job. People are motivated by what they hope to achieve in all aspects of their lives. These aspirations are very valuable because, unlike other motives, they aren't temporary.

As people approach the top, self-actualization motives lose their association with a particular side of life. Just like the main pyramid of Chichen Itza, higher passions merge into a pinnacle of highly personal and powerful aspirations—supreme determination. Let's take a look at each converging side of the pyramid.

Figure 2.2 Main Pyramid at Chichen Itza

The Forbidden Side, an Intimate Slope

The first side is too intimate for a leader to climb with others; like the first side of the pyramid at Chichen Itza, this side is a crumbling, dangerous slope that is forbidden to guests. There are no barriers or ropes keeping visitors from exploring the fourth side; most visitors see the danger and stay away from the edges themselves.

If you want to be seen as a respected leader, you must also recognize those intimate, unsafe areas in people's lives and steer clear of them. Learning someone's motivations is not about being inappropriately intimate or overly accommodating. Attempts to solve intimate problems in a business setting, such as offering to lend money, trying to solve marital disputes, encouraging time away from work for completely unrelated pursuits, and so forth, are dangerous areas for someone seeking long-term influence. If intimate issues come up in a business setting, they should be referred to experts. If someone you work with asks you to help or use resources to solve intimate issues, the Chichen Itza metaphor will help you explain your limits. Be honest about the areas in which you can help and in which you can't. Do, however, discuss any personal, less intimate topics affecting the person's work. Move the discussion away from the intimate side by asking the person about related, appropriate personal aspirations.

The Personal Side

Personal ambitions are often what an individual places the most value on outside of work. We are not talking here about unrealistic dreams or casual hobbies, but about determined pursuits.

Any given salesperson usually has one to three big pursuits that go far beyond interests or hobbies and into the realm of self-actualization. These might include spirituality, family, community service, or other endeavors.

As I did research for this book, a few of the personal pursuits that salespeople described to me also included investing, real estate, elder advocacy, competitive gardening, architecture, and education. A lot of salespeople like golf, but liking golf is not what we are talking about; there is a big difference between a scratch golfer who makes an annual pilgrimage to Scotland and someone who plays every two weeks in the summertime. A business-meeting golfer has a hobby; the "old course" traveler has a pursuit.

Does trying to tie personal endeavors to the work at hand drive results? Yes, but you have to look at this from the other person's point of view or it will seem trivial—this is anything but trivial if you are the one with the passions. Let me give you a few examples of how Sales Blazers are able to integrate personal pursuits into the sales effort. In the process, their support, and their teams perform better.

Samuel, a Sales Blazer at a firm that provides medical technology, increased the course of revenue 40 percent, then repeated the feat four years in a row. Samuel consistently finds ways to use people's passions and self-concepts to create deeper motivation.

Take someone from Samuel's team who has a passion for martial arts and envisions himself as a Tae Kwon Do expert. Mediocre sales pros would see no connection between Tae Kwon Do and progressing sales. But an astute Sales Blazer like Samuel asks how some of the tenets of Tae Kwon Do, such as discipline, preparation, channeling energy, and daily consistency, connect with the daily drive that a potential project or a sales week requires. People who believe that these principles are part of their identities regard them not only as principles to live by but also as purposes for bringing excellence into work goals. Such people respond well to the language of the team or of the leader that challenges them to apply the principles in specific ways on the project. The team's cooperation improves, clients' next steps gain checkmarks, and individuals thrive. Salespeople's early starts skyrocket, homework is thorough, focus improves, and daily cold calling increases. As a result, performance spikes.

James, a Sales Blazer at a business products company, is a master at championing individuals. He also increased growth to 35 percent, while counterparts continued the 8 percent trajectory.

"James is a master of employee relations," an inside rep said. "He understands and assists in my personal goals."

The phone rep was excited about educational opportunities in his personal pursuits, such as financial investments and real estate. The support person's interest in investing was more than a distraction, a hobby, or preparation for retirement; it was a determined pursuit. The amount of time, money, and emotion it takes someone not only to learn but also to succeed with these investments in volatile markets is astounding.

The financial principles learned are profound and often universal, even applying to what would normally be considered unrelated to sales opportunities. Leaders like James are creative enough to make pursuits contribute to fitting sales opportunities instead of becoming distractions.

These undertakings are often surprising. The person that Marie is currently trying to influence collects early American brilliant-cut glass. This pursuit is part of the individual's identity. Unique passions are a significant part of what individuals pursue and of how they see themselves now and in the future.

Another Sales Blazer, John, helps individuals as he helps his company succeed. One of the people he is trying to motivate to the next level has a passion for endurance running. It would make no sense to encourage endurance training that cuts into work time, but it does make sense to apply to sales the careful and consistent measurement of input, tempo, output, differing daily workouts, and results that endurance runners are used to.

John's colleague thrives on the physical and mental strength developed through endurance running. A great leader, John is creative enough to connect sales steps and endurance concepts of tempo and scheduling scientifically detailed workouts—the very work habits any leader hopes of a support person or slow-moving colleague. Challenging yourself or others to use the same principles to plan and execute work is sparking a performance pursuit. Unlike a hobby, a pursuit requires consistent, disciplined work, continuous focus on detail, and investment to achieve. A great leader reinforces this universal ethic by relating the investment with success in the work at hand.

William accesses these types of motivations with each of his people. Although he emphasizes the usual analysis, activities, and results, he does more. William becomes familiar with and helps the performer pursue personal goals in life if he can creatively find overlapping goals, ethics, or practices. He strongly encourages freedom and creativity inside normal job responsibilities by offering a job consistent with what a person values.

William, a real motivator, recognizes what his people value and rewards their successes. One rep says that to make the personal approach work, William pays attention to people, not just to profits, and makes it "appear easy, but [he] really does much

59

behind the scenes." Does tapping personal passions produce? William's rep says it does, because William brought his company out of "trouble and loss" by achieving over 100 percent growth. In a company that had lost direction, William "created this revenue stream that ignited the firm." His accelerated growth was "significant" to his company's success.

The difference between a person's interest and a valued pursuit is the investment in time, money, and emotion he or she makes. A hobby is an outside interest; self-actualization is a passion within. It is a passion to go beyond. Some of the lower steps on the personal side of the pyramid include financial pressures, retirement, loved ones, and social circles. This strategy isn't about taking the time to become everyone's best friend; it's about learning people's passions at all levels so you can weave them into a performance pursuit.

The Career Side of Chichen Itza

Career ambitions transcend the current job. If you've been at your company your whole career, you may not see the difference. If you've switched companies a couple of times, you may see your job and career as very different with only a small overlap. Sales Blazers champion the higher aspirations of both types of motivations to spark performance pursuits within everyone they must influence to create career performers. They tie career motives—for our purposes, to become expert sales professionals—with their performers' personal side of the pyramid to help them become accomplished people.

"Some salespeople see the ultimate progression to CEO, some to a sort of territory CEO, while others to the most valuable national rainmaker," notes Daniel, a Sales Blazer with several growth successes at DFS. Others have a unique passion for becoming experts in relevant, niche areas, and envision becoming consulting sales professionals, building C-suite relationships using their highly developed expertise.

"This is how they see themselves—from this perspective, progress is limitless."

Top salespeople sometimes have more job and career security than support people, marketers, and other salespeople below them. As a result, Sales Blazers trying to lead a cross-functional team in a long sales cycle don't always experience the same needs, thoughts, and urgencies about career as other members of the team do. Salespeople acting as project leaders during the sales cycle can easily lose sight of the exciting financial and motivational impact specialized assignments, titles, contacts, or training can have on the career opportunities of others. They might not think about how much the career plans of others can affect experiences with certain prospects and customers if the relationships are harmonious.

> *Too much, or too little attention:* If a salesperson senses that a leader is ignoring his or her future needs, the rep will bolt. Likewise, if someone thinks a salesperson is pigeonholing him or her into one type of future, that person will seek a new home that allows more freedom.

Some progressive companies have set up talent markets, in which talented people can negotiate job transfers, obtain development opportunities more easily, build networks, and develop intangible assets. Career consideration done right doesn't lead sales and support people out of a company if the company is clearly willing to continue to meet colleagues' needs better than anyone else. Besides improving revenue growth, attracting and retaining motivated people is really what this strategy is about.

Exploring the career side of the pyramid may begin with learning an individual's vision of personal compensation in the future, or résumé bullets still missing, career-building contacts, or industry recognition. Salespeople are constantly and specifically trying to clarify these and will spend time fulfilling them if the company doesn't help them achieve their long-term goals. Sales Blazers pick up where their corporations may have left off. These leaders realize that using career ambition to motivate is the easy part; what takes a little more creativity is unleashing powerful personal ambitions to provide that extra surge of direction for work done well.

> *A different focus:* Mediocre managers press for numbers and closes. Sales Blazers take the time to learn each individual's higher aspirations and then emotionally champion the person's cause. Instead of "prodding or pulling on the reins," they hold on for the ride.

The Job Side of Chichen Itza

Is it possible to use personal goals to motivate others and still increase revenue? Yes, but the real spark happens when we put the aspirations to work on the job, not just when we discover what the aspirations are. From a salesperson's perspective, his or her deepest aspirations, both personal and professional, converge at the top. The Sales Blazer commits to learning each person's aspirations and combining them with the year's sales pursuits. Can managers with formal reporting structures afford to focus away from the numbers—the goals of the job? Sales Blazers don't take their eyes off the numbers, but they focus just beyond them. Salespeople are often more ambitious and have more profound personal and professional pursuits than the general workforce. A Sales Blazer realizes that commissions come first, but that a year that is successful in capturing that extra margin of growth has purpose beyond just money.

I have to admit that this observation conflicted a little with my previous selling experience. Not just commissions? Really? Yes. We have all probably overheard conversations like the one I heard a gentleman named Wynn have. A sales manager, he was engaged in a phone call with his rep while sitting next to me on the airport shuttle. He spoke loudly on his cell phone. He sounded as if he were headed back out to visit the field.

"I know you're new, but $5,000 a week just isn't enough," he said. "You have to realize that I have a rep bringing in $35,000; another bringing in $25,000; and everyone else is calling in with at least $20,000 a week. You have to raise your level of thinking. You've got to bring it up or this isn't going to work out."

After ending this conversation, Wynn called someone else. "I talked to her and told her she needs to get that number up. She's new; I'm pushing her as hard as I can," he said.

It sounded like the cold, hard sales world I was familiar with. I thought, "That poor guy's approach is going to end both their careers." I wondered how his competitor improved results. I did empathize; he had to bring up his numbers. But with the desperate approach he was using, I imagined that one or both of them would be gone before the next quarter. It's difficult to direct a thoroughbred by chasing it.

I went back to a few Sales Blazers to reconcile what had seemed like a "best practice" of harping on salespeople's numbers with the holistic approach of putting the numbers in personal perspective. Jon, a sales manager who spent more than a decade in wireless data and communications, thought he saw a better opportunity with another network provider, but ended up disappointed. I asked Jon about leading numbers or people and about the seemingly soft emphasis of this strategy.

"I left my new management job after a short time because all my upper executive did was pound and pound on numbers," Jon said. "That's all we were—a number. Life's too short. Besides, growth comes in bursts that way. The only time I've ever thrived with a team is when I've hired people who were headed somewhere, learned what really got them energized, and then helped them use their personal motivation to do their job well. We'd target skills needed for their next level or promotion, and I'd help them work toward it.

"I know there are managers and companies out there who totally reject the idea—dismiss it as too soft to actually impact growth. But it's not like we replaced sales goals with this; it was in addition to all the other work we were doing. With 65 reps, it was definitely a process, but I saw it pay huge dividends. I think that more and more, the great companies are embracing the personal approach."

Regardless of our titles, if we aspire to lead we must be willing to be responsible to maintain the job side of the pyramid and prevent it from crumbling—to lead within the overlap of goals for the person's department and the individual's aspirations to create a spark. If we don't communicate how our requests further company *and* individual goals, we lose trust with the organization and the people we lead. Sales Blazers can be observed continually strengthening people's roles so the steps are a clear and a solid way to the top of Chichen Itza, where all four aspects of life converge.

Can you help lackluster performers reach personal goals, too? After a heroic effort, in the worst case, formal managers may have to help these people find the goals that overlap with another company's sales job—it would actually be disloyal to keep them in a bad fit. For informal leaders, such a suggestion would clearly conflict with the person's department goals. Luckily, dealing with lackluster performers isn't often necessary. Like the horse trainers said, "Most like to run."

Is there any other support for understanding how to weave together personal and professional goals? Again, the answer is a resounding yes. Let's take a look.

THE PATH TO PURSUE—INTERNALIZATION

Goals are critical, but if you can't motivate yourself or your people to emotionally internalize sales work, you haven't sparked a performance pursuit. What does it mean to internalize goals? Herbert Kelman, social psychologist and professor emeritus of Harvard University, did work that helps explain what it means to internalize work. In a nutshell, the key to his findings is this: Workers chase profound needs (as discussed); we, as leaders, can influence them to deliver more of what we need by making the job deliver what they need.

Internalization is the process of making the job deliver the higher needs we discovered with the Chichen Itza analogy. A powerful change occurs when people internalize their work. They adopt it as their own mission, as part of achieving deep, personal ambitions and values. When a leader uses internalization to influence people instead of asking them to achieve someone else's goals, the results are better.

Internalization means tailoring a job to individuals' personal pursuits in order to help them achieve your work goals, similarly to how Terry, Debbie, and Loren do with horses to get them to perform. Getting performers to see the job as their set of aspirations and a way to realize profound pursuits is what Sales Blazers do.

Note the progression up the face of Kelman's findings in Figure 2.3. The stack on the right face of the graphic shows a progression. Internalization produces better results than compliance or identification with a leader or sensible task. What is advantageous for a busy leader with a lot of people to lead is that internalization doesn't require "babysitting" to get a performer's highest-quality effort, as some other styles do. Internalization never goes away. Work becomes a pursuit by performers for their own deepest needs. Performers drive themselves with determination. (The three concepts on the left side of Figure 2.3 are discussed in a later chapter.)

Like Chaquita heading home, salespeople's efforts can take off by involving personal initiative. We learned about each salesperson's deeply held motivations while discovering the three safe sides of Chichen Itza. Now it's time to stop using compliance to get salespeople to identify with our goals and us, instead inserting the goals into their purpose in life.

Driving to success with more than money or threats was the part of Bo's story discussed in the Introduction that was most impressive.

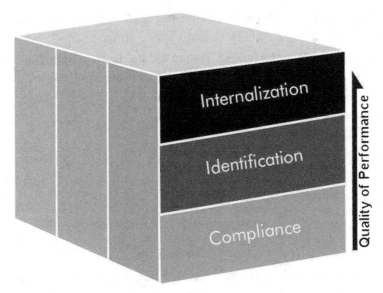

Figure 2.3 Herbert Kelman's Influence Process

"We started working right away, but because the goal didn't seem reasonable, there was a journey that I had to go through before I could truly impact my team," Bo said of his most recent growth year. "I did some tremendous soul searching. I had to examine everything. I also had to find out who each salesperson was and what they could believe."

With his "insane" goal of over 28 percent, he said he had to find a way to reach above and beyond the number and himself, and do it quickly.

"We all had to realize this was about something bigger than the number," he said. "It was about us. We all had to believe for belief's sake; it wasn't the product or just the money. There were livelihoods at stake.

"I had to believe there are good things in life allocated for me, and then I had to get my team to believe that too. I had to maintain perspective as I did my soul searching. Belief became a very big part of my life as I was going through this, because that was what it was going to take for me to truly stand up in front of my team and say, 'This is what I'm asking you to do; I'm asking you to believe when, without closer examination, it doesn't seem possible.'

"Sure, my team has been very well compensated, but money couldn't have delivered that number; it was going to take soul searching on the part of each individual to find his or her own reason to believe and to strive."

More Than Maslow

Weaving purpose with the job goals sparks something in the salesperson that is far more potent than pressing a person into compliance or enticing with money alone. In Figure 2.4, you can see that internalization is the only way to reach the salesperson's highest needs. Money only goes so far.

How do we spark the new purpose and determination that Chaquita demonstrated? We sit down and offer a vision of how

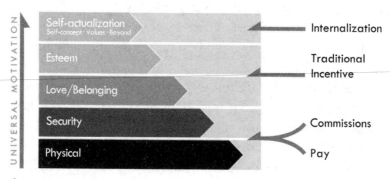

Figure 2.4 Employing Maslow and Kelman

the year ahead can deliver deeply personal and professional aspirations. When people realize that coming to work means heading somewhere they have always wanted to go, it starts a powerful reaction, just like turning Chaquita's head toward home. The conversation helps the people realize that there is now more time, resources, and friendship available to help them achieve more than they ever have before. It's the same job, but the salespeople now adopt it as their own pursuit and do it better. Directing vision toward personal possibilities is the spark that ignites a performance pursuit.

Sales Blazers seem to understand internalization instinctively. I heard a consistent refrain: "As I go beyond the numbers to help you achieve what you want, you help me increase growth along the way."

When Sales Blazers learn the aspirations of people, their approach is not entirely charitable or entirely self-serving—but it is respectful and genuine. These leaders call it a "symbiotic relationship." Consider Richard, who leads transportation contract sales, for example. His team raced sales from zero to more than 25 percent growth, boosting the top line an additional $6.5 million. One salesperson reported how revenue grew because Richard stayed so aware of what motivated each person—whether it was a certain goal within the family or a personal pursuit—with fervor.

"It's easy to forget what being in the field is about," Richard's rep said. "Managers like Richard learn what makes people tick and know when to take the company hat off."

"I spend at least one hour per direct report per month discussing personal and career goals," another leader said. "It is very important because then I work to contribute to these goals."

Sales Blazers use motivations to keep purpose behind the day's and the year's performance; they learn to make the job a set of passionate pursuits.

Think about how you would feel if your leader knew what you were really after in all areas of your life and could really get behind some of your ambitions. Consider if he or she found several ways, not just commissions, to help you get there. Consider whether you want your people to move like Chaquita when they arrive at work tomorrow morning. So, how, exactly, do you spark a performance pursuit? Turn your Chaquitas toward their Chichen Itzas. Let's look at a step-by-step approach.

THREE STEPS TO SPARK A PERFORMANCE PURSUIT

Sparking a performance pursuit calls for a leader to take three quick steps. Again, this strategy doesn't add new hours to the leader's overloaded schedule. It simply adjusts some of the content of conversations with people over lunch or during one-on-one meetings.

First, the leader has a Chichen Itza Chat with each salesperson. He or she discovers all three accessible sides of the pyramid to understand the most important needs of the individual and what each person was born to be. This may span several conversations.

Second, the leader finds a path to the pyramid by weaving personal and professional goals into the job—internalization. The quota the salesperson needs to carry changes from the destination to an incidental load.

Third, to create that spark of passion, the leader must engage each person in a formal conversation whose goal is to direct each person's sight toward home. During the conversation the leader describes how the person's personal and professional goals may be reached on the job and with company resources and points out how the specific principles, excitement, and expertise from an individual's ambitions and experience can apply to the position. Sales Blazers find the path to what's important to their colleagues and then turn their colleagues' heads so that they can see the way home. Leaders ignite the awareness that these people's jobs include reaching the top of their own pyramids and by doing so they have sparked a performance pursuit.

Key Examples of Performance Pursuit in Action

Tina Zitting, district manager for Avon, recently ramped to 15 percent growth while counterparts achieved 6 percent. She's stayed in the top 10 percent growth for several years. Her success in the South earned her a transfer to pick things up in the West. She got to work and reached number 1. My observation of Tina at work with her salespeople reflected the approach of the other Sales Blazers. I watched a meeting between Tina and Mandi, one of Tina's salespeople, and noticed immediately that their discussion about Mandi's kids' upcoming activities wasn't an icebreaker; it was serious. I asked Tina about it.

"I get to know their personal goals, not just work-related goals," Tina explained. "Then I make a real effort to partner with every one of my people to find a way this job can help them make the goals happen. There are some salespeople that don't know what they are after; they just deliver. But most know what they want to achieve."

Tina told me that the only way to reach success in business over the long term is to reach success in life. Part of this is taking seriously the effect her job has on other people. And because of her position, she has to accept and even embrace that she is partially responsible for helping her colleagues succeed with anything that work touches in any way.

Tina's expressions made it clear that she wants to bring other people to their version of success.

"If you help others reach their goals, your goals will be met," she said. "I start every single conversation by getting an update, whether it's on the kids or where they're headed. When we sit down, I make sure that these are things we talk about. If they do not already have these kinds of things in mind, I help them develop them. It's totally worth it. Finally, I translate what I need for sales or what the company needs into how he or she can reach a piece of his or her own goals, at least long-term. Then we talk about my assignments to help get there—we make a plan."

Mandi, the rep, summarized the reaction of salespeople to this approach. "She is a master of the individual. I would move mountains for her because she's always behind what I'm doing."

I saw a similar meeting the same week while working with a sales force automation company, but this time the meeting between manager and rep covered the personal and then proceeded to talk about career goals in an amazingly open, comfortable way. The leader then proceeded to discuss briefly his own role in making progress—no empty promises, just championing steps. I saw and heard about these conversations over and over among Sales Blazers. A sobering question is whether we show this much interest in the people we try to influence.

Is pointing out the path home to Chaquita ever risky? Yes; but Scott, a Sales Blazer selling software for an enormous company, gave an example that shows even a difficult path can work.

"Sometimes this is a long-term thing," he said. "I had hired a guy from a services organization in his late 20s with a new family. He was a smart guy who knew how to sell but he kept saying, 'I wish I could just go off and make chairs.' I would have given him a pink slip but he was one of my best people."

The rep was committed to Scott and he was selling. But the rep would go away to Alaska and then another place to make a serious effort to refocus, and within two weeks of coming back he would be in the same spot mentally.

The next time the rep said he wanted to just go make chairs, Scott asked, "Seriously, if you weren't doing this, what would you do?" Scott told me that the rep was young but was in the midst of starting a family, and he needed to figure this out now.

"You figure out what your real backup plan is . . . not some dream, a feasible vision," Scott said to him. "As you do, don't think about this building, this company, this marketplace, or this industry. Figure out what it is you would really do if all this went away.

"He spent time and he decided that he would go back to school," Scott explained.

Sometime later, the company downsized after an acquisition; the rep was still a top performer.

"You're never supposed to lose your top performers, right? You have to be careful with this, but this guy was miserable," Scott continued. "I was going to downsize, and so I approached him. At first he said, 'What are you telling me; you're firing me?' I said, 'No. I just want you to think about it. If you're not happy and this job is killing you, I can make the landing a little softer with a financial package. I don't have anyone who isn't performing and even though you're at the top, you're not happy. Just think about it.' He came back to me and said, 'I'll take it.'"

The "higher ups" tried to get the rep to stay, but he said, "No. I'm going to do this." He'd been raised an academic. He went and got his master's in psychology. He wasn't working for two years. Now, he's just finishing his dissertation about executive coaching and he's getting a Ph.D.

"I hired him back a year ago," Scott said. "He's happy and selling better than ever because he uses what he loves; he's helping our executives and, more important, prospective executives, succeed. He was a critical part in winning the biggest deal my area brought in last year. He has a great career ahead of him. He'll end up at our corporate headquarters and is already in our mentoring program helping our VPs become SVPs. I got him back better than ever because he chased what he needed to, and we're the ones who helped him see the possibility."

THE DIFFERENCE

Whatever you learn about your own aspirations or those of your people makes you better at influencing your people than your competitors are. A performance pursuit is a powerful path home because it isn't temporary, like quota checkups. The salesperson tenaciously earns company revenue as part of a much bigger quest and relationship. Everyone wins when you spark a performance pursuit.

WHERE THE STRATEGY FITS

Before summarizing this strategy, it is important to know where it fits in the Sales Blazer Method. It's the second of the first three strategies—the preparation strategies. First, we prepared by removing problems threatening growth; then, we prepared to lead by employing deep, human motivation with those we lead. Can we use what we have learned to spark momentum with prospects? Yes. Next, we'll expand what we've learned to prepare to pick up the pace with key prospects and avoid competitors—we'll get something called the express pass.

Strategy Summary—Spark a Performance Pursuit

1. In your next chat with a team member, scale the five steps of Maslow's Hierarchy of Needs. Remember to discover all three safe sides with a Chichen Itza Chat and genuine intent.

   a. Start by exploring the career side of the pyramid, asking:
      i.   If you could pick any livelihood, what would you pick?
      ii. What's the next step to solidify your personal specialty?
      iii. What professional groups do you belong to?
      iv. What particular awards/certifications have you won?
      v.   What's your ultimate professional goal?

   b. Do the same for the personal side:
      i.   Tell me about your home and your dream house.
      ii. You have everything under control; have you always? Describe your life after hours.
      iii. Tell me about your family or loved ones.
      iv. Have you ever won or led anything outside work?
      v.   Outside of work, what things do you invest a lot of time, money, and emotion in—more than a hobby?

   c. Later, remember the rep's job history together to contemplate job enhancements, including:

      i.   Was there a job that just didn't put food on the table?

      ii. Were there ever jobs in which you didn't feel secure?

      iii. When did you feel like you fit in the best?

      iv. When were you most valued by your company?

      v. What do you want to be best at in the future?

2. Scan the Web and brainstorm with others on how a portion of the person's pursuits can be woven with the work.

3. Explain the opportunity and the boundaries to each person and champion the pursuit of the overlapping needs. See www.salesblazers.com for Chichen Itza tools.

Get the
Express Pass

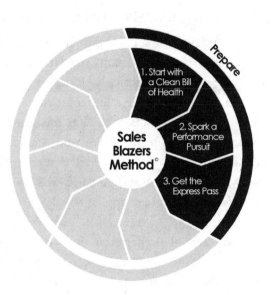

THE STRATEGY

Do more strategic, earlier preparation and influence key accounts to preempt the competition—*Get the Express Pass.*

What we will accomplish in this chapter: We will define the preemptive strategy work needed to get something called an express pass. We will review how specific preparation preempts the competition. We will learn to influence sales directly by using the Sales Blazer Method with prospects.

THE PROBLEM: ONE SALESPERSON GETS THE BUSINESS

It sometimes surprises sales professionals to see that other people are squeamish about talking to strangers, especially about something valuable. Similarly, it often surprises Sales Blazers to find that rank-and-file salespeople may be squeamish about learning whatever it takes to win business. For some people, accelerating a relationship is uncomfortable, even if the intent is genuine. Sales Blazers recognize that only one vendor gets the business, and two-way familiarity is how it happens. The *Get the Express Pass* strategy applies to salespeople and leaders at any level.

This third strategy of preparation overlaps two frequently taught selling skills: doing key research—homework—and building relationships. We have all been on important sales calls where we were embarrassed by the lack of preparation and relationship building that had taken place before the meeting. We have probably even been guilty of this ourselves once or twice.

Aaron, a vice president of sales for a major chemical company, described this problem well from both sides. "The preparation side has always been something that I've focused on," Aaron said. "It's amazed me how you can see both sides of preparation. You see the account rep who takes you to a key account and gets lost on the drive, which is always telling, or doesn't quite understand how to even get in to see decision makers. I've seen where really key things are happening in a business and an account rep hasn't done even ankle-deep homework. It's embarrassing, and it's disempowering. I mean, you lose the ability to play the part of a supply-chain partner when you don't understand the dynamics."

Sales Blazers don't rely on their presentation skills or titles to influence prospects. They don't try to know everything about every account. They learn the right information early and get familiar with decision makers of key prospects without taking control of accounts alone. They expect teammates to do the same. Together, the right homework and accelerating relationships resolve poor preparation; they qualify teams to get the express pass, which we discuss next.

> *Two parts to preemption:* Sales Blazers build a culture of winning by doing the right preparation, and they establish rapport directly with decision makers without trying to be heroes.

THE SOLUTION: GET THE EXPRESS PASS

Theme parks have a special pass that allows certain groups to go to the front of any line. Groups can arrive early to buy this express pass. With a little preparation and sacrifice, the entire group is permitted to cut in front of long conventional lines, just in time to get on the rides. As the express pass holders squeeze in, the throngs that have been waiting wonder, "Why do they get to go first?"

You can get an express pass in sales, too. An express pass in sales is a preference given by prospects that moves you to the front of the vendor line. Preempting the competition is the essence of the express pass. Preempting means helping your people displace the competition and seize key accounts with two major ingredients: better homework and leader influence.

Aren't doing homework and building influential relationships two different strategies? No. The *Get the Express Pass* strategy is to be first in the prospect's mind at the right moment. It takes the right homework to build a relationship and the right relationships to get to the real story. And it takes both to preempt competitors.

The park express pass: Mass marketing the pass would go against its purpose—to limit access. The right people must be asked in order to find the subtle location of the pass.

The team that plans ahead, makes sacrifices to do the right homework, and invests in relationships is invited to the front of vendor lines, right past bewildered competitors. Sales Blazers don't make excessive investments. They do the right research to create the influence that makes the difference in the sale. The right preparation and the right relationships with the right contacts get them and their teams the express pass.

Does doing homework apply to small, transactional sales too? Observation of transactional sales leaders revealed that when they understand business issues better than the contact does, the contact starts to rely on them. In other words, it isn't just about the complexity of the sale; it is about the relationship and the contact's desire for the team's influence.

Does the leader really affect the sale? Observation of mediocre managers and Sales Blazer managers showed clearly that leader influence is key. Lack of a relationship between a manager and key contacts, or worse, a manager's overbearing control, can derail sales. Instead, a personal, balanced approach with contacts in a coordinated partnership with the salesperson wins sales.

PREREQUISITES BEFORE BEGINNING HOMEWORK AND BUILDING RELATIONSHIPS

Before discussing how to do the right homework and accelerate relationships, it is important to note that there were two prerequisites to which Sales Blazers committed. Sales Blazers who set out to get the express pass committed first to investing a little time early and consistently on strategic prospects, and, second, they planned competitively. Let's take a look at each prerequisite individually.

Invest a Little Time Early

You have to show up early to get an express pass. Sales Blazers I observed and worked with invested up to 15 percent of their time, depending on the industry, in one or two *strategic accounts*. What's a strategic account? A strategic account is one that, in addition to the normal, probable prospects in the pipeline, will be more important if it can be won. Some strategic accounts are currently key to competitors, and some, if they can be won, will create revenue ripple effects that are larger than usual.

The goal is to cultivate a couple of key prospects over time in order to accelerate the ripening of the opportunity. Don't get stuck in the office or working only on urgent matters. Invest now so that when the time is right, you will be ready, and the prospect will decide to give the business to you before other competitors have even knocked on the door. Remember, preempting is the essence of the express pass.

Plan Competitively

The second prerequisite to doing homework on and building relationships with prospects is to plan competitively using a meaningful strategy. Strategy was born for the battlefield and then brought to the boardroom. When the word is applied to beating competing reps, it regains a little of its original bite. Sales Blazers think through a quick field-version of competitive strategy. They consider traditionally strategic factors such as the strengths, weaknesses, opportunities, and threats (SWOT) of competing reps, not just the organizations they represent. By doing this as a team, Sales Blazers project the future fit of prospects with the incumbents and identify gaps that they can fill.

Sales Blazers precede their homework on strategic prospects by developing a vision of the competitor's place in the contact's future. The team prepares an alternative vision for that future. Investing small efforts early to understand competitors' fit with strategic prospects helps preempt more passive competitors when the current vendor ceases to fit.

Scott, a Sales Blazer at a leading software company, is a great example of thinking strategically. He was brought in to lead a struggling team at a new company. By year two, the team had increased business by 40 percent. Scott offered a key competitive insight.

"Strategy occurs at all levels of an organization, especially in the field," Scott said. "What's most important is to understand your specific goal and the means available to achieve this goal. Strategy came from the field of battle, where it was used to attain a goal by understanding the adversary, surroundings, and resources available."

The field, where the actual competition happens, is where SWOT information is powerful. Scott takes competitive preparation very seriously. "I love military strategy," he explained. "I use those principles to win competitive deals with my team by learning the strengths and weaknesses of competitors and utilizing all the assets of my team and company. In a few select accounts, we've intentionally targeted a large competitive installation with the primary objective of elevating our position while weakening our opponent. In most cases, the long-term outcome is a complete competitor displacement."

With the commitment to understand competing reps and to invest a little early and often in strategic prospects, Sales Blazers preempt competitors' opportunities to remain relevant to the business. Now, with prerequisites in place, how does one research strategic prospects efficiently and accelerate relationships? Let's take a look at what it takes to get the express pass: the right homework and an influential relationship.

HOMEWORK WITH A JOURNALISTIC ZEAL

The Goal of Sales Homework: The Inside Scoop

Get the inside scoop: Discover the hidden needs of key prospects before and better than competitors. While investing early in strategic prospects, Sales Blazers show *journalistic zeal* when doing their homework. For key prospects, successful salespeople learn the details and finances behind "who," "what," "where," "how," "when," and "why" that are not available to competitors. The public story is often a set of facts that you can read about in press releases, but decision makers usually guard a more private version of what opportunities and pressures exist and what they are thinking and feeling. These competitive details, hidden in the minds of the contact and the larger organization, are the inside scoop. Where do we start digging? Naturally, with "who."

All of us in sales have heard countless times how important it is to identify the right "who"—the decision maker. We have also been conditioned to consider the CEO's perspective and the people who can influence the deal. So, how do we weave all this together? A key part of doing homework is research—asking the right people the right questions. What do we ask? We already know the types of questions to ask. It turns out that having a Chichen Itza Chat—a discussion of the questions about powerful, permanent needs described in Chapter 2—is an effective way to get the scoop. More specifically, a Chichen Itza Chat can be redirected to identify the personal, career, and job needs of two people who are not yet on your team: a member of the prospect's executive team and your contact (see Figure 3.1).

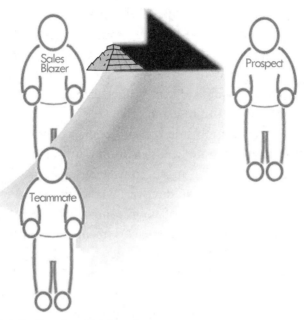

Figure 3.1 Redirecting Chichen Itza

In a Chichen Itza Chat we ask important questions about five areas of need on which all people focus—physical, security, belonging, esteem, and self-actualization—and we identify these needs from personal, career, and current job perspectives—three sides of life. We also avoid the intimate side, with appropriateness as our only guide. We work to learn the unique version of these needs for individuals we hope to influence. We want to get inside their hearts and minds to find out what they are really after and to create new momentum.

Learning the Chichen Itza priorities of the relevant executive and your contact is compelling. The perspectives and specific needs you uncover translate easily into selling to a large corporation or even a small group. All that is necessary is to uncover the priorities among securing key assets, available cash, people, revenue/expense, and mission needs in the respective context. However, the power of the early version of a Chichen Itza Chat is more suited for individuals. In this chapter we will focus on corporate context and research.

Discovering the job side of both contacts and their executives' views of corporate needs yields unique selling opportunities. We discover the most convincing reasons for a key prospect to buy when we discover overlap in the needs of the company and the needs of your contact on the job side of Chichen Itza. Doing our homework to understand the job of the firm through its executive leadership and the job of our contact will get us the real "what," "where," "how," "when," and "why"—the inside scoop. Let's take a closer look at learning about executives' needs on the job side.

The executive of the prospect that is relevant to the sale varies and might even be the CEO. This person understands or shares priorities with the rest of the executive team and the larger firm. The needs of this executive help us get his or her unique view inside the heart and mind of the organization—the places where budgets shift. Interestingly, the most important needs of leadership and of the people that make up a company can be mapped directly to our Chichen Itza learning. Let's consider how these areas of need map for an organization (see Figure 3.2).

What are the physical needs—or critical assets—the organization requires for success? Critical assets include buildings, new equipment, strategic patents, agreements that grant unique access to markets, and other things that provide the basis for the organization. All these involve significant invest-

Figure 3.2 Chichen Itza for a Firm

ment. Public Web sites and annual reports offer hints at what these key assets are, but what are the more specific, pressing answers, and how can we quantify financial impact? This requires more digging, which we'll do a little later.

What provides security, ensuring a future for the company? Cash flow is what keeps an organization solvent. Investing this capital ensures a healthy future for the organization. Large, strategic investments of capital have different freedoms and constraints than expense budgets have. What are the specific capital initiatives at the key prospect? Solutions that affect these initiatives are another large source of spending for strategic investment.

What are the belonging needs of the organization? Without people, an organization is simply a set of legal documents. Employee and labor expenses are often the single largest expenditures for an organization. Cultures determine which people stay and how well they perform. Initiatives and cooperation are how the work gets done. Performers and CEOs desperately need, not want, to have the right leaders, people, and teams doing the most critical work. What key initiatives involving people promise incomparable impact, dynamics, power shifts, and sales opportunities at your prospect? Budget moves quickly if it moves people's performance.

Where does an organization gain esteem? Nearly every organization is judged by measures of managing revenue increase and expense decrease. Each effort is recorded and potentially ranked for specific line items; we only abstract this into an ultimate profit number. Is there a new initiative that your offering could enhance in some way that would directly affect sales or expenses for the better? Such purchases often escape drawn-out, abstract debates about return on investment (ROI) because the result is so obvious.

What are the organization's self-actualization needs? In other words, what does the company need to do to perpetuate its purpose? It takes every effort to fulfill a vision with a mission. Customers—the people served by the organization—are only half the story. The awareness and benefit of the larger society in the company's mission is always critical to the organization. The prospect's specific projects to take this purpose into the future in a big way—the vision—usually resonate with the executive purse holders. We must learn how the executives see these needs.

It would be difficult to find anything more important to a prospect and to the people that move their company forward than the answers to the Chichen Itza questions on the job side. If we can get specific answers to these questions about important initiatives of the firm from the executive's perspective, we will be in a position to help that decision maker do the job. Addressing these answers with our solution goes far beyond simply offering features.

Now for the important part: Imagine for a moment that we can quantify the financial impact of these executive priorities for the firm and then uncover how our contact's personal work contributes to these needs. Let's look from our contact's vantage point at his or her basic needs on the job side of life and see how he or she might view things.

What work is our contact engaged in that is most likely to provide for his or her own *physical* needs—bonus, commissions, and raises to put food on the table and pay the mortgage?

What work could our contact do that would create job *security*—make him or her indispensable in fulfilling one of the company's important needs?

Belonging? What change in an initiative would allow our contact to associate with more people and higher titles throughout the organization and engage in satisfying teamwork?

How could our contact gain *esteem*—quiet appreciation of the CEO, or public recognition or an award? Most likely it would be to make a clear, visible impact on a critical need we have identified.

How could the decision maker *self-actualize*—achieve his or her valued goals—by finding overlap in his or her unique purpose and the company's purpose, and then furthering both dramatically?

What would happen to the length of the sales cycle if you, a new resource, took the time to help find overlap between (1) executives' efforts to fulfill company needs, (2) your contact's

SALES BLAZERS

job priorities, and (3) ways you could help fulfill those needs?
My guess is that the sales cycle would collapse into a mandate
by your prospect's executive team. Add the personal and career
answers of a full Chichen Itza Chat for your contact and executive, and you would undoubtedly find some powerful motivation related to your sale that you wouldn't have seen otherwise.
Imagine how this insight would change the language you use
with the prospect and how what you say would move the sales
cycle forward.

Let's look at a couple of examples. The first illustrates that
"who" is really two people: your contact and the executive who
understands the goals of the firm. The second example illustrates how fulfilling significant corporate needs should really be
"what" you are selling. These two insights set the stage for
learning the rest of the details.

First, consider how one Sales Blazer with a $15 million
quota and the recent top growth ranking in his company
emphasized that "who" he serves in client organizations is not
just his contact but also the relevant executive who is aware of
the most important company needs.

"I keep who I am serving and how I further the company
needs in mind when serving my clients," he said. "First, I am
here to further the goals of my prospect's company by meeting
the needs of the executive involved. This person is important
not just because he or she can sign a purchase order but
because of his or her awareness of the most pressing company
needs. Because my day-to-day contact is also my client, my goal
is to help him or her personally succeed. There is no better way
to do that than by fulfilling a critical organizational need. Both
people—the contact and the executive—are important to our
collective success."

This veteran salesperson spoke in terms of how he and the client could absolutely succeed together. He said things like, "I know we can because I've been doing this for 30 plus years—my programs will have a tremendous impact on the two individuals and their company."

As he championed the needs of client organizations through executives and his contacts, a trusting partnership developed.

"I want them to know that this isn't just so I can make money," he continued. "It's to help their firm, their management team, and ultimately to help them as individuals. You have to make sure that people really understand that you care about their success and their company's success."

Once you have figured out the "who," discover "what" the success should look like by exploring the details of all the basic needs. Scott, who led a cross-functional sale to a large hospital, offered this great example of the powerful "what" that homework on the job side might deliver.

As you read Scott's story, keep in mind that the goal is to try to find more than one area of overlap between the most important job needs of the contact and the executives of the company. Note how Scott's team ventured beyond the need that their industry traditionally fulfilled—people initiatives—to affect initiatives in two more areas of need.

"We met our contact with a general hospital," Scott remembered. "The rep had been developing a trusting relationship, but the time had arrived for her to do business with someone."

Scott described how the contact expressed the desire to do an extraordinary job—to "knock it out of the park" with this new project. He also remembered the rep's sense of partnering.

"It would have been easy for the salesperson to go it alone with just the contact and present software, process, and product advantages that we have. We wouldn't have won. Instead, it became a team effort to uncover harder-hitting needs to beat the competition."

Scott described the usual talk about workforce initiatives that he and his competitors have with clients. Then he described how in this case they wanted to create more impact. They quickly found an opportunity to improve the financial market's esteem of the hospital. A hospital increases revenue by raising "bed occupancy"—the primary unit of sale in a hospital. This part was obvious, although the competition hadn't made the connection to revenue explicit. Scott's team dug deeper to discover how the organization was trying to boost bed occupancy.

"The clearest path to increasing bed occupancy rates is bedside manner—essentially great customer service for patients," Scott said. "We connected how our solution could do just this—improve bedside manner. Then we made the connection to revenue. The importance of bringing together a team who could speak about our solution in terms of improving bedside ratings and occupancy rates was key."

Affecting bedside manner directly would do wonders for bed occupancy and our contact's job—contributing to her hospital's revenue need—and ultimately to her career. Speaking about system features strictly within people needs wouldn't have worked, because this happened to be their competitors' strength too.

"Our message wouldn't have rung as true to our contact or her committee as a differentiator," Scott said.

The team had started with people needs that were predictably tactical because that was what their solution was built to address. They'd uncovered revenue needs that were urgent. The team also sensed they could help drive strategic organization values—they could help perpetuate the purpose. So they learned about the nuances of the hospital's purpose from its executives. They asked how the hospital's position on *healing* and caring was different from that of other hospitals. They spoke about the real priority within the hospital's values. All the homework and dialogue uncovered the corporate version of self-actualization—some primary values the hospital was trying to become and to communicate to employees and to the public.

"The team learned ways the prospect sent this message throughout the workforce and community," Scott described. "We learned ways they perpetuated this purpose. This kind of language was throughout our proposed program. We showed clear ways to create behaviors that would send their particular message of healing and caring in powerful ways to patients and ultimately the public. Understanding the important nuances instead of just the day-to-day needs of the contact was key in winning this deal."

Scott described the contact's gratitude for the team's thorough understanding of the hospital's three important needs and of her role in fulfilling them. She felt gratified as the program was launched publicly and satisfied at a job well done.

This story explains clearly the importance of doing great homework on the "who" and the "what." However, the "why," "where," "how," and "when" are important details that cannot be forgotten.

There is one huge assumption in gathering all this information: that we have access to all the right people and to all these great insights. If we can gain this information directly from the source, we know that there is a high level of trust in our relationship. However, trying to get answers to these questions even before meeting with the CEO and decision maker is often where we need to start. Now that we understand our goal, we'll take on the challenge of skirting the company's public story about these needs—or worse, the company's silence—and get to the inside scoop.

Homework That Gets the Inside Scoop

Sales Blazers win competitively by providing the first and only detailed answer to how the prospect can meet the needs that have been described, and when they do so, they reap financial rewards. To communicate this fit, salespeople must do some digging to understand the needs as clearly as their contacts on the other side of the table, with no assumptions; in other words, salespeople must do their homework. Homework delivers the real picture; the real picture delivers real commissions.

So many Sales Blazer observations involved exceptional "homework" or "preparation"; it is clearly a differentiator.

As one leader said, "I, like others in sales, have had countless experiences with companies who said, 'The reason we selected you is because you really understand us and what we need better than anyone else.' "

Am I suggesting that we all become research analysts? No.

Darin, a former consultant with McKinsey & Company, and a proven entrepreneurial business executive, warned, "Even when selling consulting, you don't sit and study everything there is to know about the company. You're not trying to know everything the decision maker has in his head after 30 years of experience. Instead, you need to spend your time getting to the heart of the key issues quickly. You have to understand the real pain and the real solution and what immediately surrounds it better than anyone else. But you do have to find this first by looking broader with a quick hit on the basics."

There is no one better at unearthing an important, hidden story than an investigative journalist. A reporter who relies on partial, public facts goes hungry. In contrast, the investigative reporter who fills in the real story first wins awards.

> *Investigative connection:* Breaking a large, inside scoop first is everything in investigative journalism. It's also everything in sales.

John Maines is an investigative reporter for the South Florida *Sun-Sentinel*, best known for his IRE (Investigative Reporters and Editors) Certificate Award for his breaking story on FEMA (Federal Emergency Management Agency) fraud. A judge for this award called his investigation a "standout." It "detailed fraud and abuse nationwide that cost taxpayers more than $530 million. . . . The specifics are shocking."

Sensing a Potentially Large Opportunity

John and his colleagues sensed a story about questionable FEMA expenditures while investigating a supposed flood in Detroit in 2000. John, a research expert, noticed some irregularities and went to work. The story reflected sales in important ways.

At the beginning of our first discussion, I said to John, "The difference is that salespeople don't have time for a lot of extra research."

John surprised me by saying, "I don't either. I guess our goals really are similar."

It turns out that the standard who, what, when, where, why, and how that reporters learn in Journalism 101 is actually more about quick thoroughness than excessive, exhaustive research. As John pointed out, "A good investigator gets through that initial list of research quickly and thoroughly." Rather, it's about sensing where there is an inside story to be told and getting the real story filled in first.

With the FEMA story, John said, "I started with the Web, pulling public documents, newspapers, and news releases to see what exactly had happened. We looked quickly at everything we could possibly think of, including talking to every official we could for information. How many fire trucks went out? How many pumped basements? How many police went out to guard flooded roads? The sorts of things that would happen during a flood. And the answer was, 'None!'"

> *Focused investigation:* Getting the express pass includes quickly scanning public sources for related issues with an investigative zeal but without overresearching. The goal is to assess the key needs of the company and of the decision maker to identify, not the public version of who, what, where, how, why, and when but the inside answers with the most impact.

John said he knew he was dealing with a real story, but he didn't know "what was really going on." He described doing what we do in sales. He said, "I'm doing analysis to fill in the blanks, to see what money went to each location and who got it and why, and what it paid for and how they got it. But I wasn't there yet, I still had a huge void of what exactly happened."

A Qualified Opportunity but a Partial Picture

Does John's style of leading his team's research really apply to sales? Absolutely. The dollar amounts are larger government numbers, but see if what he describes next about the competitive money trail and filling in the real story sounds familiar.

"I think the best example of getting the inside scoop goes back a ways. When we saw that $168 million went to Detroit for FEMA aid back in 2000, but there was no storm and they had no real flooding problems, we wondered how it could be possible to get $168 million in FEMA money when you had no serious damage," John noted. "We knew FEMA inspectors had been in, so we had many questions.

"Maybe the police just didn't respond? Maybe nobody bothered to pump out the basements? I could say $500,000 went to this neighborhood for new television sets that were supposedly damaged in the flood. But how does a television set get destroyed with no flood, and so many of them?"

> *Limited access:* Prospective clients view some information as fit for the masses, but some facts remain guarded on a need-to-know basis—there's a public version and an inside version of the story.

What John explained to me next was really the reason I had called him in the first place. I asked, "How would you solve the age-old problem of getting around the wall of silence to get to the real story?"

"Right; that's the question," John replied. "How do we find the facts that change everything just as it might in sales?"

To get around the silence, John asked himself an important question: "Who else might know about the pain and would talk?" Some people can't help but talk about their opportunities and pain. Those who rub shoulders with the people with the challenge may talk about the real story. John called these people "end users," to connect with the sales analogy.

The concept that end users and decision makers have both a public and a private version of the story explains a lot about how sales calls go. As John said, "In our business, we're trying to find out problems that our end users' bosses don't want them to tell us about."

I told Dan, a divisional vice president of sales in Europe for Nova Chemical, about John. Dan described to me the exact same phenomenon in sales.

"You know, there's always an arm wrestle, a bit of a tug-of-war, that goes on with information," he explained. "Every customer you deal with knows information is power, so you're always negotiating for the middle ground of information. From a procurement point of view, a procurement officer—a good one—wants as much privacy as possible, so I don't know what the key drivers are to profitability. I don't know how much value my product is really delivering to them, and what their risk is of losing me as a supplier."

Dan described how a good procurement officer tries to build a wall guarding certain facts—usually the important facts. The good salesperson, on the other hand, tries to get around that wall and create "transparency, not to the point necessarily that procurement sees everything on your side, but to the point that you know what that customer's hard-hitting needs are and what the switching cost is for them from competitors or if you walk away from the process."

A great source for the inside scoop: In sales, investigating who has contact with end users is critical. End users can often illuminate the private money trail—issues and paths to decision makers—more readily than purchasing or lower-level evaluators.

Dan pointed out the need to start by finding people who will talk. Dan's teams uncovered real stories to grow his $500 million division and gain him a promotion back to the United States. In the United States, he ricocheted his new division's $6 million revenue into an astounding $100 million.

End Users Tell the Inside Story

"The end users, the affected, are the ones that will talk more than officials," John said. "In my story, the people paying the money were the government and inspectors, but the end users were the poor. Some wouldn't talk and some didn't even have a telephone."

So John did something key. He got out in the field; he went to end users at different locations who were in the same situation and got around the silence.

John found similar end users in Cleveland. He said, "In our business, we try to find the names of people. We pay a visit wherever we can and just talk to them a little. Maybe we get a name of somebody in the office, even a secretary sitting at a desk instead of trying to get around them, or we find out who works there, maybe from their Web site, employee of the month, you know, and we call them to start."

John is professional, but he does what it takes. He explained, "We may have to try to get them outside of work; every business has a common place where people go out to lunch. We might casually walk outside their office building with them when they're leaving. You would be surprised, if you know just a little of the real story, what you can get people to talk about."

John wasn't suggesting ambushing people or being "creepy"; he was just suggesting asking people to help solve a problem and learn about the person who knows the most about the issue.

"You can say, 'We're trying to find out as much as we can about how you guys handle this,' or 'Can you tell us how your existing XYZ system works?' You don't stop here either; you keep digging," he said.

"In Cleveland," John continued, "I'd called city officials who should have received calls about the floods. You know, 'You're a lousy councilman, my neighborhood flooded, why can't you guys fix the sewers?' They didn't know anything."

So John went to Cleveland and talked to businesses about the floods there in 2003 and 2004. He talked to people and their neighbors. He talked to clergy who would have been involved with giving aid to people.

"You know," he said, "everybody comes to church on Sunday and half are flooded, the clergy would have known about it—they would know the end users. I kept looking.

"I talked on the bus," John said. "In Cleveland, for example, a city bus is a big thing. They'd be riding the bus. I asked,

'Did you have a flood here last year?' [This was in 2005.] I was in a real dangerous neighborhood and people just stared at me, you know. 'How about 2003, do you remember a flood?' They'd just stare. So I'd ask, 'Have you ever heard of FEMA?' Finally, someone said, 'Oh, yeah, those guys, you mean, Santa Claus!' and they'd laugh."

"These people went on with stories about how you do this," John said. "They said, 'Oh, yeah, FEMA comes in, you just tell them a little story, tell them a little lie, and they'll send you all kinds of money.' They talked of telling friends saying, 'Say hey, you know you could get this money, the FEMA sends around an inspector to see if your TV is really dead, but he barely looks.'"

John pointed out, "It is surprising how well the grapevine works. We also investigated the Miami-Dade claims, which started the whole FEMA investigation with the 2004 hurricane in Miami. The hurricane never hit."

> *A better source for the inside scoop:* Users at a different location or who are involved but not ultimately responsible often tell the real story. Talk to prospects about the product they're currently using that you're trying to replace, issues they face. Get answers to how key initiatives affect the flow of assets, investment, people, revenue, expenses, and how they might or might not perpetuate the purpose of the organization.

The stories John heard from the Miami-Dade people about faking damage to property were identical to the stories he had heard in Cleveland. In both places the people had said, "You use the garden hose to spray down your sofa. You spray soda pop on the walls to make it look like the wall was flooded. You unplug it or smash it or something like that." John noted, "From Miami to Cleveland, the same knowledge is spread, and boy does it spread. It spreads like a wild pandemic."

Other Organizations

People living with a situation, even at other organizations, may fill in the blanks that purchasing doesn't.

"Suppose the company doesn't want your salespeople rummaging around talking to their people," John inserted. He suggested that there's still a way to find what you need to know. Try finding out about the product from another organization that uses the same product, understands the prospect, and might be more cooperative. For example, a small company that is friendly with the prospect might be a little more helpful in connecting powerful organizational needs to your product or service.

John continued, "Usually, whatever problems are going wrong in one place are also going wrong in another. For example, I'm basically a data analyst who deals with other reporters. I have certain problems that naturally come up at work that I don't bother to talk about. When I go to a conference, I talk. I talk to the people who do the same thing I do—my version of your end users' groups and trade shows, I guess.

"In a way, these people from different cities know something about me and my company that other people at my company don't even know," John said. "It's that network effect again. So you're not necessarily stuck trying to talk first to the people you're selling to."

Is a user group or trade show trip worth going on for access to every prospect? No; but how about for strategic prospects? Yes.

Decision Makers That Are Suddenly Helpful

Remember, prospects might find it "uncomfortable" if you are "snooping" around. One lesson is that the closer you get to finishing the puzzle, the more help you'll get, even from those who wouldn't help before. For example, John went back to Detroit, and people talked once he knew much of the story. John said, "If end users sense your awareness, they feel safe and are suddenly willing to talk about private, hard-hitting issues and how smart they are. They give names freely and even help identify dollars impacting the problem."

What It Takes to Get the Scoop: Zeal and Sacrifice

I asked John if he could ever write his stories from his desk. He said, "If I sat at my desk and looked on the Web some more, would I have found the FEMA problem? No way. It wouldn't have worked. Instead, I thought, 'I'm going to go into those neighborhoods.'"

I asked if it was dangerous.

"It was," he said. "I was nervous, but it's my job. I could get shot at and make people mad. Yes, there were gang fights going on in the neighborhoods. I just had to be careful."

Given my perspective, I naturally thought, "John's walking near shootings? At least we never get shot at literally in sales."

"I think if salespeople's leaders could get teams to try talking to people, they would find they have great results," he reasoned. "Believe me, it was a pain, but it helped fill things in. In retrospect, it was a fantastic result. I came out with the real story by getting out on the streets, getting away from my desk."

Using Journalistic Appeal to Get the Express Pass
- Answer who, what, why, how, and when using the investigative format of the Chichen Itza Chat.
- Talk to end users and others who are familiar with issues and with decision makers.
- Revisit decision makers, who may now be more willing to help.
- Prepare to tell a story of how your solution fits in with the decision makers' most important needs.

Examples of Getting the Scoop in Sales

I worked with many enterprise software and database salespeople—Sales Blazers—from Oracle. Glenn, a well-respected regional manager, has a group of professional salespeople who prepare. They expect one another to learn everything about a client in order to make a sale. When asked how realistic this type of preparation is, Glenn replied, "Are you kidding? If our salespeople start reporting on an account without the specifics *and* without a relationship with the key contacts within an account, the sales team is able to see the gaps quickly. They better really know the needs of every decision maker who touches every opportunity within that account."

Chris, from IBM, agreed: "Salespeople are expected to develop a long-term relationship of trust with the customer—influential contacts and the C-level executives."

So what does journalistic zeal look like? One Sales Blazer of a supplier to the transportation industry illustrated the importance of journalistic zeal well.

"The decision maker of a huge transportation prospect was a VP of operations who had a strong relationship with our competitor's rep," the leader recounted. "We got them buying a few of our small products, but we could never get in with this guy. We needed this account. We needed to understand how this guy saw things. Our contact had said this VP was very smart, but from other vendors we'd heard that he sometimes made emotional decisions."

The leader set out to research what was important to this decision maker and what his vision was. He and his team made some phone calls to people they knew he'd worked with at other companies. They heard two scenarios: either he was bright or he made emotional decisions because of seemingly pet projects. What they were really hearing was sometimes the decision maker paid attention to purpose as much as finances.

"Our task became to see if we could get this guy to make a good emotional decision in our favor," the leader said. "We had also discovered that he was passionate about homeland security after 9/11 and how all his vehicles around the country could help while operating normally."

They finally got a lunch with the decision maker and the VP. They planned to discuss how their company could be a more valued partner instead of just offering piecemeal products. They even found a friend who actually knew someone very high in Homeland Security. They found a way to connect on a higher level of Chichen Itza.

"At lunch, our VP explained, 'There is a way we could help you with your vision.'" The team explained that they were connected well to Homeland Security on a particular initiative. They explained that they could make this a priority and even had the best supply of some of the products.

"The prospect was on the fence before the lunch; after the lunch it became a slam-dunk," the leader said. "We had that deal done in four days. If we hadn't done any homework on what was important to him in his business, if we had gone in there with only the basics, we wouldn't have gotten the business. Sometimes the decision maker has subscribed to the view that your particular offering isn't business relevant. You have to know how you can provide every value available in the relationship."

Dan, the chemicals sales leader, agreed. He said, "If your customer is tied to what's happening in the pulp market or in the natural gas market, the account wants to know you are aware of all the energy market variables that impact their business so you can be an empathic listener and supply-chain partner—that you are there to help them be successful. The most important thing we do is to take the data points and create a hypothesis that we can present to the customer to get them to fill in the blanks."

The inside story and listening: Why listening is still underrated: Even the flashiest proposal is only as good as its comparison to how the competition's proposal fits the inside story.

Dan explained that simple awareness matters. He said he was fascinated by how many salespeople don't even listen to a quarterly conference call from a key prospect's CEO. Salespeople who will actually tune in to a Web cast and listen to a prospect's CEO will find out more information about how they can bring value to that account than the contact sometimes knows.

"The most brilliant thing I see," said Dan, "is salespeople who are able to take all the relevant data from talking to the customer's customer, understanding the market they're in, and understanding the company's earnings or news releases and creating a competitive hypothesis for what the switching costs are, and what value they can bring. That's power in negotiation."

As John, the journalist, said, "The trick is to fill in the complete story. That's what I'd do."

After doing your homework with journalistic zeal, you have to use the information to build a valuable relationship—valuable for the client. There are two prices for the express pass. The first is homework with a journalistic zeal to deliver a new, better inside story. The second is to establish an influential relationship with the decision maker.

INFLUENTIAL RELATIONSHIPS

Displacing competitors doesn't happen without a trusting relationship. A trusting relationship is really how you complete the new inside story, and vice versa. Sales Blazers build a relationship with contacts in coordination with others who are involved. What these leaders do can be described as accelerating a trusting relationship by offering a piece of themselves and other resources. The question is whether one can really accelerate the development of genuine trust in a new relationship. After working with Sales Blazers, I now know the answer is "Yes!"

In the Beginning

Most people who are masters at accelerating quality relationships have a difficult time articulating how they go from stranger to true friend so quickly. It's a difficult task—a little like explaining how you accelerate the aging of a good cheese.

A great example of accelerating trust comes from Tom, a sales professional who covers all of Manhattan. As we have discussed, we all have a unique passion for one of our talents. Tom's is accelerating the aging of a good relationship with prospects.

"I love developing relationships with people," Tom said. "To be quite honest, this passion is probably the thing that's kept me in business for 32 years. Clearly it wasn't my moderate IQ or because I was a B student. Relationships with clients for me are what it is all about. This passion for getting to know new people is where it starts."

Tom warned me that he wasn't rehashing Relationships 101 by suggesting next that you begin with the other person by pronouncing his or her name correctly. Growing global diversity means that we are all exposed to names that are more difficult for us.

"This means more than ever," Tom continued. "The most beautiful sound a person hears is their name pronounced correctly—especially by a new friend. It happens so rarely."

Tom related a story about the smile he saw on the face of the chairman of one of the largest companies in the world because Tom was one of the few salespeople who got his "difficult" name right when they were introduced.

"With names, it isn't a matter of degree," Tom pointed out. "You practice and get it right or you don't. When you say the name, the person either feels like you know each other already or they feel like you don't. Pronouncing someone's name perfectly is the initial relationship accelerator."

Next, Tom explained that you had better have at least your Web homework done on the individual before ever shaking hands.

"My sales mentor, a gentleman named Norman Tanner, taught me that your clients' interest must become your interest," Tom remembered. "You must find a potential common bond that is meaningful before saying hello the first time."

To move a relationship into friendship requires experiencing things together, which provides more time to chat about the important things.

"You have to realize you're not going to get there in the first five minutes," Tom said. "We trust and learn a little at a time. We may be talking about the second visit or phone call before we get to experiencing things together."

The second meeting may present a moment when it is appropriate to share a piece of yourself within the common ground if you have built trust.

"As soon as they ask you a little more about yourself, you know you've started the beginnings of a relationship," Tom explained. "Obviously, you keep the focus on them. A note or a short call of a personal nature can do wonders. Thursdays and Fridays aren't just great days because we're heading into the weekend. Thursdays and Fridays are great days to safely ask, 'So what are you and your spouse planning for the weekend?'"

The Thursday or Friday call is when you can invite the prospect to share an experience of common interest, perhaps even with family. "Oh, you were thinking about going to that? My wife and I have two extra seats and we'd love you to sit with us."

"But let's be honest," Tom confessed. "Sometimes when you call on people, they only have ten minutes. They're curt and impatient—'Just the facts because I've got to get going.' If you haven't started at the top, the relationship might just be a smile, a warm handshake, and an offer to shorten the meeting to five minutes, to share that you empathize and have something very important—results clients have experienced. But let's face it, sometimes you have to try three or four doors before you get through."

"Finally," Tom concluded, "With the tough ones, I always make sure I leave before they have to say, 'I'm sorry, I've got to end this now.' From my perspective, if you don't, you instantly become a vendor instead of a developing friend, and people prefer to buy from people they like and that they trust, even if it takes a while."

Offer a Piece of Yourself

Like Tom, Dan often brings a little of his personal life into a deal to build relationships. He remembered, "One account we struggled with was a company that operated in central France. It was a very large, very key account. We really wanted to break in there, and we knew the guy had a love for skiing. Our company had an annual customer seminar at a ski resort, usually a long way from France. I knew wining and dining wasn't enough.

"We invited this guy's boss, the owner of the company, a few times, but he turned us down. One year, I was determined to get this owner, Bernard, to the event. I sent him ski information, snow reports, comparisons between Alpine powder and Rocky Mountain powder (which he'd never experienced) and, of course, I involved my account rep. The problem was, he didn't speak English very well, and I didn't speak French. My French account rep couldn't come—very few salespeople from Europe actually attended."

Dan grinned and said that he has a brother who is fluent in French and who also skis. Finally, Bernard agreed to attend.

"I arranged for my brother to accompany Bernard and his wife," said Dan. "My brother was to act as our host and ski guide for the day. On our very first ski run, my brother, the ski expert, blew his knee out on some challenging terrain. Poor guy."

Dan was afraid his whole plan was going up in smoke. "But as it turned out, and this will sound strange, it was one of the most endearing things for our relationship," Dan explained.

Together, they all helped Dan's brother get down the slope, and they got him to the ski patrol.

"We still have contact eight years later through Christmas cards and the occasional phone calls," explained Dan. "After that visit, Bernard became a great customer of ours. We still maintain a strategic-level supply position at that account. Every time I talk to Bernard, it's 'How's your brother?' Although my plans didn't turn out exactly as I wanted, the fact that I'd offered part of me (and my brother's ligament), instead of just skiing or some small gift, made their experience meaningful and it worked out perfectly."

Sometimes, adding a second relationship, such as with a manager, can bring a sense of teamwork and trust to accelerate things.

A Second Relationship

Bringing together other people to help in the sales process is discussed in a later chapter; however, presenting a partnership between salesperson and manager or executive brings something besides expertise. The leader's title and ability to provide access to resources gives clients confidence in the salesperson's ability to marshal necessary resources for the business side of the relationship.

A Sales Blazer named Jim is a good example of partnering with reps and bringing resources to bear. Jim created a boost in ad sales by increasing placements by 28 percent or more each month in a market that was declining. A seasoned, high-income ad-sales rep told us that Jim made the difference in deals by bringing all the learning, teamwork, and leadership together. He gets things out of the way of deals and gets to know contacts personally. Jim works to gain a clear definition of problems and opportunities through gathering facts and knowledge. He then works with the team to "plan the execution jointly and follows up to see how things are progressing." The salesperson described Jim as a leader who gets involved with clients and brings resources to the table to help clients see opportunities.

"He's a hard worker who facilitates progress through challenges," this rep said.

Like Jim, Sales Blazers are partners, not parents, to salespeople or lower-level contacts. It's okay to talk to each other about this before a crucial visit. People don't appreciate a leader who grabs the steering wheel in a relationship. Building a bond with decision makers must be done in partnership. Likewise, creating additional relationships within the prospect's organization must be coordinated thoughtfully and done with respect.

Dan echoed this important consideration about building relationships, which I heard from many.

"A salesperson doesn't want to feel disenfranchised at an account," Dan said. "A lot of groundwork has been laid for a relationship with the prospect. The worst thing that a leader can do is go in and say, 'Okay, now somebody's here that can really negotiate this.'"

Dan explained that the procurement contact doesn't want this, either.

"I've watched with interest as a procurement officer, who is the main bread-and-butter contact, watches all the attention focus on his boss as soon as the boss arrives," he said. "You may meet with a procurement individual who feels very estranged from management with a very hierarchical approach. The president of the company may join the discussion. If the contact leaves feeling undervalued and with an attitude, it's probably because of the guy he brought in, but he'll transfer that resentment to your company."

Dan explained that a leader's job at that appointment is to know with whom he or she is meeting, to know where that person fits into the hierarchy, and to bond with everyone, no matter what his or her level is.

"There's a need to make sure that, even if the president or the CEO of the company is coming in, you continue to acknowledge, direct conversation to, make some eye contact with, and build the value of that procurement guy to his boss," he explained. "Then you'll achieve a win–win. If the procurement person sets up that meeting with his or her president and all you are doing is disempowering the procurement person and giving all the attention to the boss—brass-to-brass, that's a bad call."

Not only can sales leaders' genuine (or disingenuous) intent be sensed as they talk, but so can their actual ability to help.

Build Confidence by Marshaling Resources

Leaders and salespeople who bring the right tools and other resources together in a critical moment are impressive and often get an express pass. This marshaling gives decision makers and contacts a vision of your uniquely beneficial and available capabilities as a leader.

Scores of Sales Blazers were observed "taking action using company resources" or "getting resources freed up to make the sale."

One Sales Blazer in human resources services said, "The key in bringing the right resources is to make sure you understand who each contact in the account is and what they are after, then, bring the right resources to bear for each."

Marshaling resources early can sometimes get you the express pass, as this Sales Blazer says, because "by targeting and bringing in the right resources, you show that you have listened. You are showing you are interested and capable of solving the problem, not just making the sale."

Sales Blazers marshal the resources for them and their teams to create self-sustaining capability. Impressive and timely marshaling is often the difference in a sale because it is seen in stark contrast to the aloof leaders of competing teams. The risk people run if they don't understand the situation is throwing every resource possible and hoping something good happens, yet missing the main issues altogether. The leader needs to choose and attain the right resources to address the key issues.

One leader who wields resources skillfully to develop relationships is Mick Fox. Mick lit a fire under AlphaTech's previously falling revenue to get it back up over 35 percent growth.

"Revenue had been falling monthly," explained one of Mick's coworkers. "In six months, Mick led a revenue reversal and ended the year with over 35 percent growth and a profit turnaround."

Mick, like so many successes, doesn't just show up with a standard marketing message. Mick focuses on the entirety of the customer's situation, not just his own product. For example, he builds relationships with contacts not just by staying in constant touch but by adding significant value during each conversation. One client asked him about shortcomings with their financial software. Mick's not even in that industry, but he arranged for the right tools to be brought in to solve the problems. Because of his ability to marshal resources, he's viewed as a trusted advocate, not a peddler. The point is that Mick didn't stand to gain anything directly by helping the client outside of his bailiwick, but he did stand to strengthen the relationship. It worked because he offered his mind, not just his product.

Mick marshals small resources, too, to accelerate relationships. He sends motivating materials to clients that focus sharply on how the client's problems can be solved to produce results, rather than just sending the standard sales collateral on his product's features and benefits. He provides others leads that have been well qualified, and he watches for any resource that could advance the relationship.

Some believe that quality relationships take decades to develop. This is not the case if you show a willingness to bring resources to bear that are truly relevant, because contacts will learn to trust you more quickly. Putting yourself out on a limb, so to speak, is like risking a piece of yourself—one of the most important resources of all—and a powerfully persuasive relationship builder.

THE DIFFERENTIATORS

One of the most remarkable growth differences I observed with Mick and others is the before-and-after difference in a salesperson's chances resulting from preparation and relationship building. Together, preparation and relationship building create an extraordinary differentiator. Mediocre sales professionals just show up. Sales Blazers bring a journalistic zeal that directly influences prospects to pass on competitors. It's difficult to change people and performance, even as a leader. However, the difference in confidence, performance, and results is amazing if you compare before preparation and relationship to after.

A situation can improve within minutes or hours as a result of the right preparation and relationship building. The combination may be the easiest source of better results. The key is that prospective clients notice the difference, too. Because they see the difference, they offer the express pass—they award you the business before they shop around.

WHERE THE EXPRESS PASS FITS

Sales is a fast-paced, competitive business. You have a lot to do. You can't afford to wait in line; you need to invest in an express pass. To get the right information and build the right relationships, you need to know the details not just about the people on your team but also about your prospects and their inside scoop. With obstacles out of the way, it is time to grab the express pass, the third of the preparation strategies, and preempt the competition. In the next chapter we will use the information we have gained from the first three preparation strategies and engage a team for attack.

Strategy Summary—Get the Express Pass

1. Invest time each week on strategic prospects.
2. Don't do exhaustive research; instead, dig deep for the truly relevant, inside story of the opportunity.
3. Have a Chichen Itza Chat with the CEO and your contact to uncover the inside version of who, what, why, how, and when.
4. Get around the silence of the CEO and decision maker with journalistic zeal.
5. Don't get information through end users and others at any cost, but remember that simply gathering public facts won't paint the whole picture.
6. Get to and complete the new inside story that prospects are willing to write a check for.
7. Marshal resources that are relevant to the client's needs and go out on a limb to build relationships at all levels.
8. With the right information and a relationship in hand, accept the express pass and preempt the competition.

Play Your
Depth Chart

THE STRATEGY

Build flexibility into your team so that unique team talent can be matched with unique, competitive opportunities—*Play Your Depth Chart.*

What we will accomplish in this chapter: We will discuss how traditional, rigid organizations can sometimes get in the way of team results. We will define a depth chart and explain how this organizational strategy matches talent to team opportunities. We will learn how to make flexibility and ownership coexist using a depth chart approach. We will see the context of this strategy within the others.

THE PROBLEM: ORGANIZATION SET IN CONCRETE

In training workshops, the *Play Your Depth Chart* strategy is often introduced with a question: "Why does it take a football team 30 seconds to make wholesale substitutions and reposition for an opportunity, and it takes businesses six months to a year?" The answer lies partly in the fact that sales teams often inherit or create rigid organizations, basing assignments strictly on geography, product, support, or vertical industry instead of on the situation (see Figure 4.1).

Even nongeographic assignments are often called "territories" to show ownership and avoid squabbles, commission splits, and policy breaks. The goal on most sales teams is to give very different talent static assignments that are difficult to change. But that isn't the most affective way to play to your

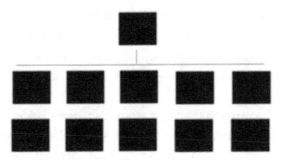

Figure 4.1 A Typical Organization Chart

strengths. The goal of the *Play Your Depth Chart* strategy is to enhance your system so it changes predictably in key situations and allows maximum results for all instead of just within each territory.

Rigid structure lets salespeople work aggressively within a territory and is seen by most companies as being efficient. But it also protects salespeople from supposedly losing opportunities they've never penetrated to other salespeople. There are, of course, sales opportunities that are fairly straightforward or small, for which it wouldn't be wise to complicate matters by having several people involved. However, each sales and support person has unique talents that may be better used with more complex situations and differing personalities. It's important to note that we're not talking here about drastic changes; we're just thinking of someone who can help when a key opportunity arises. We want to do this thinking in advance. Players in a rigid structure are rarely positioned to best use their talent, to cooperate to win the most team sales. Also, rigid organizations seldom consider help that might be available outside the team.

Tom Rhoton trains and leads channel salespeople for Altiris, a high-growth tech company. He posed a question to me: "At any given moment, are we as salespeople turning and facing each other to negotiate or squabble, and in doing so turning our back to the customer?"

The fear of trouble arising from split negotiations, channel conflicts, and other "territory complications" can stifle potential teamwork. To some, planning for teamwork doesn't seem nearly opportunistic enough. But when that big sale is lost because all the resources available weren't brought to bear on it, the manager can be forced into a hiring process to replace a rep; or a support person foresees the damage to reputation and future career opportunities and starts looking for a better fit. Either way, finding a fit for a fixed position is often followed by more turnover, because *people* do work, boxes on an organization chart don't. And split negotiations, conflict, transfers, and new hires aren't the answer either.

Tradition

Good tradition is the gradual evolution of best practice. Bad tradition halts progress for comfort's sake. A sales leader, Frances, had taken advertising and publication sales at her journal from 0 to $2 million and helped to achieve the sale of her tech start-up through her team. Top brass at her most recent sales management job told me that Frances was brought in to "shake things up" and "to bring a fresh approach to sales management." After cleaning up a few messes and getting to know the team, competition, and sales opportunities, Frances asked leadership to consider a more flexible approach.

"I could bulldoze ahead with the existing account structure," Frances explained to them, "but our opportunities have such unique business challenges and requirements and personalities that I think we could attack these challenges in a better way."

She continued, "We have a large number of what are seen by the important members of the field as equitable, named lists. These make compensation and leadership manageable, but I've seen coverage and personalities that just don't match well with the prospects. The stiff structure gets in the way of business challenges and technical needs required to win the biggest number of area sales. We also need new urgency for customer-relationship people to uncover new opportunities, and focus on where the big checks are coming from."

What Frances proposed was to divide assignments according to geographic territories but also plan ways to cooperate instead of just naming accounts, plus create a national account role to allow more of a team approach and reduce hoarding. The current top sales leader respected the suggestion. Other leadership felt that changing the long-held tradition presented too much risk. Some leaders congratulated Frances for creating an option that maintained each salesperson's compensation level and also increased fit and coverage, while others argued, "The aftershock would kill us," pulling for tradition to win. Some resonated with the new approach and tried it in their districts. They found that with a new, more flexible approach, they were able to increase quotas compared to other districts. Frances moved on to another new assignment and in less than a couple of months increased sales in a brand new business to a run rate of nearly $2 million annually.

Convention Is Comfortable for Whom?

Because I, too, was comfortable with permanent organizations' "fit with territories," I was surprised that Sales Blazers could view organization as fluid but still avoid commission-split chaos. In fast-paced sales, it isn't as simple as "getting the right people on the bus" and putting them in the right seats, which are bolted to the floor. Sales Blazers think "outside the bus" because, in sales, opportunities change every day. They build systems that enable opportunistic repositioning quickly, allowing them to attack without creating chaos.

Sales Blazers know the market, but they focus more on individual opportunities, which may even mean branching out to the entire area, not just their own territory. They see their job as helping in all the territories at once, not just focusing locally. Sales Blazers understand that accountability may mean reaching your goal, but it also means accountability to cooperate to reach broader team goals. As a minimum, when the need arises, they overlay on the existing structure a simple system that escapes tradition. They expect cooperation, they involve non-salespeople, and they make rules that allow for flexibility. The team expects to become aware of and attack opportunities with whatever it takes. They know that prospects don't really care about a team's organization; they care about being served by the right people.

In trying to discover how these leaders morphed traditional structures, I observed an intense focus on individuals. I heard things such as, "He puts me in a position to succeed," or "She found a way to utilize people's talents," and "We created a system so individuals could work together." Great leaders build a team that takes advantage of individual talents.

> *How each rep and each customer thrives:* Research has shown that assigning people work with which they have experience and that they can be satisfied by increases performance. Understanding instinctively that the team setting often makes it possible to juggle things, Sales Blazers creatively connect a sales team's talents and expertise to winning business.

SOLUTION: PLAY YOUR DEPTH CHART

What can be done to maintain accountability and ownership and still allow flexibility to attack key opportunities that arise? The solution is a system that is flexible enough to anticipate changing situations and shift talent in predictable ways.

You may be saying, "Now hold on. In sales, this is a stretch." That's okay. I've known other sales professionals and sales managers without revenue growth say that this strategy isn't realistic. So, I went back to some Sales Blazers, and one leader echoed the sentiments of many others when he said, "It's a matter of degree and just taking it as far as it makes sense. But you have to build in flexibility or you won't change results."

I watched with interest several meetings in which Hal, a sales vice president, led sales processes that included many cross-functional teams. In each meeting, as I listened to Hal, I noticed that he was leading, not dominating. I also noticed that he communicated with a respectful accountability specific to each role and individual. I couldn't help but feel as if I worked for him, and that he wanted, not needed, each person to succeed in his or her part. This made people volunteer unique contributions, unsolicited. But almost none of the people in the room even worked for Hal. His marshaling of the right people for the client was impressive.

Scott Crawford, national accounts sales manager for Pentax Imaging Company, told me a story that illustrated in its simplest form how to mold the right talent to a situation.

"Years ago I was raising capital for a start-up," Scott recounted. "I'll never forget a meeting in the World Trade Center before 9/11. The meeting was with the head of an investment-banking firm, one of the original funding sources for Federal Express. As we, the team seeking funding, walked into the corner office we were taken aback by how clean the office was."

Scott said that on the wall were many plaques with logos of companies the firm had funded. Some were draped with a black ribbon—deals gone bad. The clean plaques showed logos that were impressive. Then, they noticed something very different.

"The desk of the leader of this investment firm was clear except for an Eagle Scout medallion. Most people wouldn't have even recognized the medallion. On our team, we had Dane Iorg, a former Kansas City Royal, who had earned his Eagle Scout as a young boy."

Scott was wise enough not to try to dominate the new relationship with the head of this firm. The team let Dane and the funding boss bond, and the rest is history.

Instead of relying on Scott's selling skills, glances at the office décor, or worse, irrelevant icebreakers, they gave Dane the nod to ask the venture capitalist about what the team, representing the start-up, had noticed about the desk.

"That medallion was the only thing on the desk," Scott remembered. "It could have been his partner's office. Because the focus of the team had remained on the prospect, it allowed him to explain to us that the Eagle program had really given him his start."

The investor explained that he had hungered for structure and understanding of working with others when he was young. The medallion represented his first introduction to meaningful discipline. It taught him the concept of choosing between many and varied goals, and of achieving them with the help of others. Dane, Scott, and the team listened and responded as the man explained how he embraced the clarity of his early goals and their practical nature. He had an unusual passion even for an Eagle Scout.

"He said that he attributed his position leading this successful investment bank to that achievement as a young boy," Scott remembered. "Dane and the man discussed how the Eagle helped them model future success."

The team spoke of choosing values and guiding young behavior in each step of a career with the scouting program.

"Because his corner office was a product of this award," Scott continued, "he cleaned the office and kept this one decoration on the desk each day."

Simply introducing the investment banker to a person he could connect with made all the difference in the world to this team.

The players and positions in one situation are not always the best for another. But can this flexibility be structured? Sure. To get a great fit for talent in any situation, football teams use something called a depth chart. As shown in Figure 4.2, I have added different shapes to the traditional football version to represent unique talents.

Used in sales teams, a depth chart can organize and rank sales-related personnel according to different strengths in net-

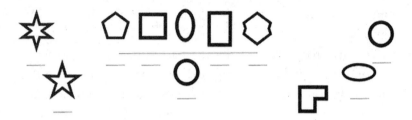

Figure 4.2 A Depth Chart

work, background, motivations, and personalities. The key assumption behind a depth chart is that people progress, and positions change, in a planned, predictable way. Each position has a set of specific potential assignments (we'll discuss the assignments in Chapter 5). Players often hear, "You'd better have the formations memorized the next time I see you." This is because depth charts require the whole team's understanding. They come in as many configurations as the myriad systems out there. The one you'll create may not resemble a football depth chart or even another sales team's depth chart. The shapes in Figure 4.3 show how a football team's depth chart is set to move and could just as easily represent varying talent in an opera, a hospital emergency room, or the particular specialties of individuals on any type of team.

"The Streak"

Early on, I realized that a depth chart was the fitting metaphor for how Sales Blazers manage to organize flexibility. I wondered if I was going to have to call in some favors to get to Urban Meyer, the father of football's new spread-option offense and a master recruiter for the University of Florida

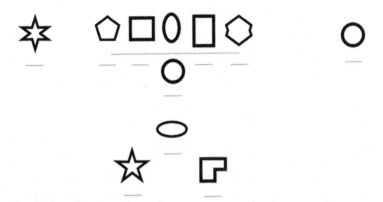

Figure 4.3 Another Depth Chart

Gators, which boast a national championship title under Meyer. Maybe I'd have to find the former assistants to the now-deceased Bill Walsh of San Francisco fame, author of a system that he called the West Coast Offense, who was also an expert manager of professional talent. The real question was: "Who leads the most successful depth chart system in history?" The answer I got was surprising.

The life expectancy of an impressive winning streak in any performance setting is generally a year or two. That wasn't true for "The Streak" at De La Salle High School in Concord, California. Their football team's winning streak began in 1992 and didn't end until 2004, when the team finally lost to Bellevue High School in Seattle, Washington. The De La Salle Spartans had the longest team winning streak in the history of any ball sport at any level—151 games. Yes, you read it right. The math is fun, considering that most high schools like De La Salle play 10 or 12 games a year. The streak included four straight *USA Today* national high school football championships and consecutive state titles. The team's story helps highlight the *Play Your Depth Chart* strategy.

As amazing as the Spartans' streak is, the approach to their depth chart is just as unique. Their system highlights the individual success that can come because of, not in spite of, assigning talent-oriented positions.

Coach Mark Panella is the person who would normally be called the offensive coordinator, but he's on a staff without titles. He runs the system with Bob Ladouceur, the head coach. Mark is arguably as knowledgeable about organizing and flexing a high-performance team in 30 seconds for specific situations as anyone on earth; he also has a sales background. Mark highlighted the importance of diverse talent, a solid system, and flexibility that translates well to sales.

Positioning the Team Members

As you consider what Mark told me about talent, systems, and flexible organizations, think of how it might apply to leading a diverse team in sales. First, he explained the importance of positioning talent.

"We have to evaluate talent," he said. "Our track record really speaks to how we put guys in the right positions to succeed. Last year, for instance, we told the guys, 'There are only two guys who have a spot locked down.' We start each year as if whatever happened in the past does not typify what this team is about. 'You guys are a new team; you are individuals. Every team's different, so how are you going to succeed?'

"Putting everyone in the best position each year gets each player the most possible playing time; they're going to be out on the field. You don't want to tell somebody that he can't do something, but you have to start by putting him in the perfect position for him to succeed and for the team to succeed."

Mark told me about a player named Andrew who, in 1989, wanted to play quarterback on his freshman team. He was 6'3", a tall, lanky kid. Andrew told Mark, "I've got to play quarterback." But Mark replied, "Move to lineman. You can start for us right now as left tackle or you'll be fourth-string quarterback. Do you want to play? If so, play tackle."

Sometimes, if a person wants to rise to the next level, he or she doesn't get to play quarterback every season.

"That's the kind of tough love that's part of athletics," Mark continued. "We moved Andrew down to left tackle, and he ended up with a scholarship to the University of Colorado, and then he signed with the Green Bay Packers. It's in the expectations. It starts right now to get them to that mindset."

Perfection? Preparing a system that anticipates change means practice. It also means planning for potential mistakes in key situations and occasionally getting temporary assignments that you and your team may not be thrilled with. Tough love also means that it is sometimes necessary for team morale and performance to cut individual performers loose if they won't learn the system and contribute.

A System

The depth chart organizes a sales team into positions that shift as needed, and it "locks and loads" substitution scenarios.

Together with the plays, the depth chart sets the stage for a working system.

In high-pressure performance settings such as football, medicine, and even the performing arts, something akin to a depth chart is part of the system. Performers learn this system their first year, and it is the same system they continue to learn until they leave the team. Leaders may enhance the system by adding more scenarios or by adjusting positions temporarily, depending on the performers, teams, and situations that arise.

It's not just a pecking order; by thinking through the various players you must lead, possible positions, and assignments-in-advance options multiply. If you understand players and competition, and have experienced a lot of situations, you can do exactly what you need to do at any time—because you are adaptable. As a leader, you can tell team members, "Here's the base system, now prepare to be called on in certain situations."

Mark spoke of knowing how to move as a team before a different opportunity arises each play.

"With our option system, everybody's got to be working in sync," he explained. "Everyone's accountable for knowing the system that we start with on day one. You're accountable to your teammates, whether you're a starter or whether you're guy number 50 on a 50-man squad. Everybody's expected to move and use their talents within the system; everyone is held to the same standards. The system is already built to provide many options even after the snap."

COMPETING TO WIN

A depth chart allows a team to change formations to outsmart the competition. Situations arise all the time in which a certain performer is just right to help bring something specific the competing rep isn't offering. We should get prepared to play in a position to succeed at any given moment without a mix-up. Sure, Sales Blazers must become a little more sophisticated to be able to make changes on the fly. But as they make their presentations following the competition with the right team, they'll win. Mark explained how this works in his world.

"A couple of years ago, we played Long Beach Poly here at Cal Berkeley," he recalled. "They were really keyed [focused] on our big-play guy, Maurice, who ended up at Notre Dame. It was his senior year. But we had another good running back, Jackie [now playing at the University of Oregon], and we knew the whole Long Beach defense was going to key wherever Maurice went.

"Freddy Parrish, their safety, knew how to defend Maurice. Everywhere that Maurice went, wherever he motioned or ran, Freddy would follow. We knew going in that this would happen, so we put three wide-outs on one side, and put Maurice in motion to the other side. You saw their whole defense just shift over to Maurice. So we threw passes to Jackie going the opposite way, and he'd rip off 15, 20 yards at a clip. By the time the competition figured out what was going on, the damage was done."

It is similar in sales. It is great when a rep, who is a phenomenal performer in his or her own respect, can succeed in a new way. Clearly, Maurice wanted the ball—just like a rep in a territory that is obviously mismatched in a particular situation will want to stick to territories. However, players who understand the system you've set up will be more prepared to do what's best. But it won't work if you haven't designed a system or if your team members haven't learned it.

Design creates tempo. If a system has such good tempo that it only takes a phone call or an e-mail to flex, magic can happen instead of chaos. You will be in a position to go right after the competition, and they won't have time to adjust to what your team is doing. The damage will be done by the time competitors finish having split negotiations, working out roles, and waiting to present formally.

RELATIONSHIP BUILDER OR WORKHORSE

Besides coaching during football season, Mark works for a Sales Blazer who is also named Mark—Mark Zierott—at National City Home Mortgage; I'll call him Zierott. Zierott's wholesale mortgage group used a depth chart approach and shot up to "top region of the year" in dollar volume.

"One way people differ is by being relationship builders or workhorses," explains Mark when making the connection to using a depth chart in the sales environment. "Zierott evaluates the people and the personnel we've got, and the type of people they may deal with: Are you dealing with people who enjoy a relationship, or are you dealing with someone who is strictly transaction oriented? What's your relationship with this prospect? Maybe taking it to the next level with a tough prospect is about the relationship."

Zierott allows his people to have some overlap in critical situations and if it makes sense. Mark said, "My manager may say that if you called on the prospect for 10 years, even though he's not currently in your territory, maybe we'll try to get a little more production out of the account because you have a relationship with him."

His manager monitors progress, and if Mark isn't able to get more business than the other rep, he carefully switches back to the original positioning. In their mortgage group, expectations of flexibility based on strength are set early. Mark explained that his manager works the other side of talent, too.

"Sometimes you have someone who is transaction oriented," Mark explained. "My manager may assign 50 prospective brokers to the transaction-oriented rep and say, 'go hit 'em.' It's always a tough call. But my manager says you sometimes have to have some overlap." He also pointed out that, in their large mortgage group, their manager avoids chaos by not just picking up the phone to start swapping account assignments before everyone knows how things will work.

FORMAL FLEXIBILITY

On rare occasions, an organization with formal flexibility is warranted. Tina from Avon said, "When I first came here, people were assigned stringent boundaries and territories. When we moved away from that as a company, teamwork and sales exploded. One part of my job that I love is matching prospective customers to representatives, and seeing it work."

Overhaul or overlay? Sales Blazers rarely call up management and suggest abandoning traditional organizational structures entirely. They show leadership by finding a system that allows them to be flexible and reach out without major disruption.

Let's look at some other ways to organize depth charts and gain cooperation.

STARS WHO COOPERATE

I observed scores of Sales Blazer managers who worked continually to get stellar salespeople to cooperate. The managers assigned their stars to help with key prospects, according to personalities, challenges, and solutions. They also asked their stars to allow others to work on an account so the team could win. And Sales Blazer team members are willing to be flexible.

"It's not always about the top performer," said one leader. "The salesperson needs to understand it's okay to ask for help—that the most sophisticated salespeople take a team, consultative approach. There may even be times when you have to take yourself out of the game for a period of time to win."

It might just be a casual phone call to offer expertise or connect understanding that makes the difference. We should constantly ask ourselves: "Would we progress this sale with just a little cooperation or, a call from . . . ?"

A depth chart lets formations shift from locked assignments to cooperation. It makes a 30-second reorganization or substitution possible without emotional outbursts. More important, it puts the best talent in front of a fitting opportunity without creating team chaos.

I asked Kim, a star salesperson I've worked with for a few years, if he reaches out and involves specialists in his sales. His look seemed to say, "Why wouldn't I if it helped the client and helped close the deal?"

"Assuming you really understand the client's needs, you reach out to any specialist who can help you," Kim responded.

"I let the client know early that I'm going to be the leader of expert resources—that I will be bringing in specialists and they will add value to the process. Then, I introduce these specialists as early as possible—the first moment I can."

Kim uses language that introduces these people in the context of what he's discovered the client needs, at least via conference call if not in person.

"Nothing lets the clients know you understand their big picture needs more than bringing the right expertise to the party," Kim said.

"Today, in the age of automation, I sometimes run into a support person who says, 'I'm sitting in front of my computer and the system says such and such a person is doing this, and that activity is going to happen,'" Kim continued. "That doesn't completely work for me. As often as possible, I get people to get out of their chairs and to meet teammates and clients face to face or at least on the phone, because this builds emotional commitment—a human connection—you can't get personal investment from a computer screen. If they know the client and each other, they will naturally be more accountable and engaged."

I asked Kim how he engages people who may not have his requests in their job description and who don't work for him formally. He said that it is critical to make specialists and support feel how important they are to you and the client, to make them feel like part of a team and to show appreciation. He also said you have to keep the opportunity important in team members' minds.

"Obviously, there are politics and structure to be navigated, but showing appreciation for people and the project is critical to keeping an ad hoc team moving together," Kim advised. "To get the right people emotionally engaged and adding their best, you're going to have to do as much internal selling as selling to the client, and you're going to have to keep doing it. You're going to have to become a partner with this team to keep accountability—weekly updates and advanced notices—flowing. Again, think of your job as doing as much internal selling as external selling and you'll get the best results."

ANALYTICAL SALESPEOPLE AND SUCCESS

Scott, a Sales Blazer from HP, went to a large software company and used a flexible approach to reverse a team's downward slide. In year one, revenue jumped to 85 percent of goal, and it reached 114 percent of goal in year two—a new trajectory. Scott spoke of flexibility as being a unanimous quality among the best leaders.

"If I have an analytical salesperson," Scott said, "I do whatever it takes to pair him or her with analytical contacts at least on key accounts. If there is an opportunity, I find a way to introduce the analytical person into the relationship. Let's be honest, many organizations don't compensate salespeople to play as a team, so salespeople don't want to do team selling. Reps don't have to have their legs tied together, but we do need to get the client the right person with the right style at the right time. If I have people with relevant industry background or style, I put them on those accounts. I find a way to make it work.

"People don't mind selling together if they know how things are going to work, and they love getting to do what they are good at; but it is a process." Scott represented a lot of comments when he said, "It isn't easy, and ironically, too much movement can paralyze results. The general approach has got to be immediately understood."

COMPETITIVE RÉSUMÉ HISTORIES

Traditional ways of organizing territories have been around for so long that most managers never consider the notion of looking back into each salesperson's history to attach the right talent to the right opportunity at a moment's notice. Jim, a Sales Blazer, parlayed his use of talent into a higher position with a second food products company. Jim's people discussed using their talents in flexible ways with him. Jim, a former employee of Frito-Lay, remembers how natural this was when he was leading a Frito-Lay sales team.

He said, "It makes total sense. It was pretty easy for me to ask someone from commercial distribution to help with the big-box buyers if he or she had the background, but it takes a little more effort to think about the personalities, and yet I know you have to do it. You also have to let people know that this is how it works: 'We're always trying to put you in a position that helps you succeed personally and that helps us succeed as a team.'

"Even in more transactional sales, our prospects like to see us as experts who can expose them to a variety of people who understand what they're trying to do. In a lot of cases, that's all we're talking about—taking a chance to show that, collectively, we really understand their industry needs, connect to their job, and can add value. Only in rare cases do we actually switch people permanently."

The point is that matching talent and styles from any-where—inside or outside the organization—to key opportuni-

> *An obvious contrast:* The mediocre sales team sticks
> to structure and knows only one or two bullet points
> on their counterparts' résumés. In contrast, a Sales
> Blazer cooperates and applies each rep's motivations
> and experience to benefit his own territory and the
> area as a whole. Leading others to understand
> prospect and competitor personalities is key. Armed
> with all this knowledge, total area sales suddenly
> become far more interesting than traditional isolation.

ties creates competitive results, but it can't be a surprise. As one
leader said, "Every sales force is different. But if I sway some
changes within our sales force, I create a precedent to bring
talent and information from anywhere in the organization,
really anywhere in our collective contact list, to close sales."

So, can you really adapt a depth chart in your area of responsibility? Let's take a look.

THE PROCESS: APPLY A DEPTH CHART TO SALES

Before you create a depth chart strategy, set aside every pre-
conceived notion about territories and compensation. Taking a
depth chart approach can range from a five-minute brain-
storming exercise to a formal system. The first step shouldn't
involve a complicated form. It should be a simple, quick brain-
storming exercise on a sheet of paper. We'll build on the information about our people, prospects, and competitors we
learned in the work we did in previous chapters. The depth

chart brainstorm involves (1) strategic prospects, (2) involved competitors, and (3) potential teammates.

Key Prospects

A manager's perspective is slightly more complicated than a rep's, so let's consider the manager's perspective in an example. Managers can't know the personalities of every individual contact at every prospect, but as a Sales Blazer, you can help. List personalities at top prospects across the top of a sheet of paper. Think about the contacts at these accounts.

Describe the challenges, personality styles, and motivations we learned as we were doing our homework and building relationships in Chapter 3. Write your insights right below each client at the top of the page as shown in Figure 4.4. For example, personality styles may include communicative, aggressive, relational, or analytical. So, under one company and contact

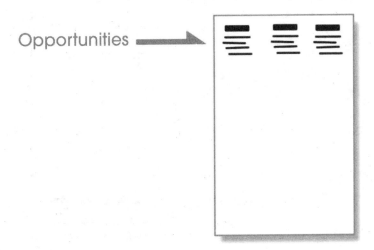

Figure 4.4 Depth Chart Opportunities

name you might write "highly analytical." But it's also important to include other facts, for example, "uses CRM (customer relationship management) software" and "thinks spreadsheet tracking is archaic." Another note might read "sold pharmaceuticals in Maine."

Salespeople's Characteristics

Write the name of each of your extended team members and that person's characteristics across the bottom of the page, as shown in Figure 4.5. Write each person's abilities and passions from previous chapters. One entry might say "biology/science," "analytical," "sailing," and "sold CRM." If sales and support people have similar descriptions, they can be stacked in the same column on the depth chart, but often they won't.

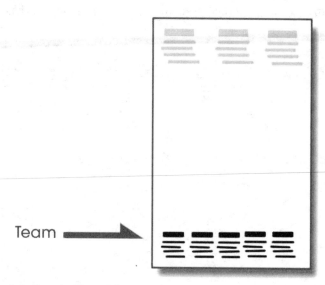

Figure 4.5 Depth Chart Talent

The Competition

The third component is competitor strengths, weaknesses, opportunities, and threats. We spoke in Chapter 2 about how strategy really gains power in the field, and about how to quickly gain information about competing salespeople's strengths, weaknesses, opportunities, and threats, and what the competition is doing at key prospects. Stack the incumbent competitors underneath each key prospect, as shown in Figure 4.6. Include strategic company and personality characteristics.

Brainstorm possible teamwork or shifts by comparing how prospects' challenges, motivations, requirements, and personality styles compare with those of each of your people. Draw lines or move your people around in different formations to connect the talents and expertise of each salesperson with the sales opportunities, and to adapt to competitors (see Figure 4.7).

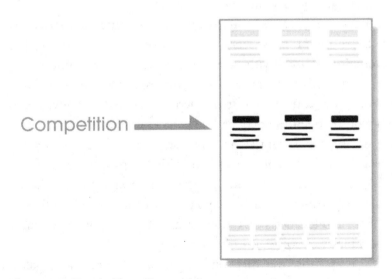

Figure 4.6 Depth Chart Competition

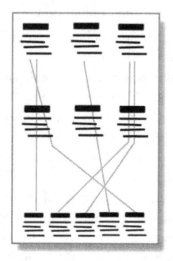

Figure 4.7 Depth Chart Connection

Geography shouldn't kill creativity; often we're talking about one phone call or someone outside sales.

Begin to see ways around competitors to tie your strengths with those of prospects, thereby making connections that weren't possible with a rigid structure. Substitution and staffing needs may appear. Think differently and more flexibly about how you can adjust the depth chart to your advantage. If you're open-minded and go through these simple steps, you'll see opportunities in your larger area that you haven't seen before. More important, individual reps will see possibilities of cooperation outside the territory and even outside the sales department. If it helps you think creatively, use different shapes and locations on the sheet, as in the football depth chart examples we looked at earlier.

You may discover that someone on your team is a weekend tycoon who stays involved with the family real estate business

Characteristics Applicable to Reps Beyond Chichen Itza

- Problem-solving styles
- Territory characteristics
- Access to territory
- Personal and communication styles
- Casual interests
- Size or complexity of accounts handled successfully

and knows real estate inside and out. The contact at his biggest prospect is a brainy individual from a pharmaceutical lab. In the next city in your area, you may discover someone with over ten years in biotech who left details off the résumé because they seemed irrelevant. Her top prospect is a national bakery chain, and she also has an account that is actually a subsidiary of SmartLabs. You may already know about a finance person who spent five years with a SmartLabs competitor, but has never sold a day in his life.

Sales Blazers instinctively find a way to connect dots like these—cross-territory subsidiaries, unique expertise, contacts, and personal style from unconventional sources. On mediocre teams, these three salespeople would never talk about contacts or cooperating, and would cling to the territory, product, or account list. The sense of ownership and fear of losing commissions would keep them from picking up the phone or passing a lead. Tradition and lack of a teamwork system keeps them from seeing any other way, fearing the resulting chaos. But a quick depth chart brainstorm and design can bring new possibilities into focus.

147

FINDING THE RIGHT OPPORTUNITIES

Jon, a successful sales veteran at GE Healthcare, spoke of finding the opportunities that fit talents on a team.

"Oftentimes, opportunities come up that require you to think and react quickly in order to win the opportunity," Jon said. "But what I've done in sales management roles is look for prospects that are companies like those a salesperson has had success with. Let's say Kerry has been successful in a high-tech company and understands the nuances and the buying decisions that might take place there."

Jon explained that it might be a good idea to develop prospects in areas where she understands how high-tech people think—where she can understand and speak their language.

"There's a lot more personal touch that has to happen with a sales leader than just going out and chasing clients all day long with reps," he explained. "You've got to be flexible enough and fair enough upfront to your people involved to understand that if situations come up that require some changes, they will be made for the better of the team."

Jon's point that we should look for new opportunities that fit what we've learned about our team members' talents is key. It would be easy to restrict a depth chart exercise to existing key prospects or an existing sales team, but it is necessary to think outside current opportunities and even beyond salespeople.

Flexing the Depth Chart without Playing with Payroll

As a manager, when thinking beyond existing opportunities and your team of salespeople, other support and sales channels should be considered, too. One great Sales Blazer, Don, remembers thinking through all the players one by one at Oracle when he was asked to turn around a struggling area.

"The first thing I did was segment the market and assign a more narrow focus for partners as well as my salespeople," he said. "One thing some people don't realize is that you have to take a holistic, team view of everyone, not just the salespeople."

An important thing Don did was to pare down and focus his partner organizations and resellers on various segments where they had specific strengths. He evaluated each person and reseller on attitude, hunger, experience, previous success, and ease of access to the territory. He asked channel partners to specialize, learned more about reps' background, and got everyone without the appropriate expertise for an opportunity out of the way. As Don put it, "You've got to invest in a team that can attack."

Don spread the accounts as fairly and fittingly as he could. He said, "But my goal was to get rid of the lone soldier mentality. Was it a disruption? People adjusted and now they actually like it. As far as salespeople go, we've had zero turnover. Understanding strengths and roles actually created flexibility when an opportunity popped up."

Like Don, Sales Blazers at all levels see beyond the sales organization chart. As one Sales Blazer said, and as several others expressed as well, "Sometimes the best salespeople aren't salespeople in a certain competitive situation."

Flexible substitutions for the team come from many sources—support roles with expertise in a certain subject, a sales engineer, individual salespeople with multiple strengths, a sales-minded accountant, even external contacts who can help make our message better than the competing salesperson's.

Defining roles that may not be permanent and setting an expectation for how changes happen create predictability

SALES BLAZERS

within the team. Each member understands his or her role and its inherent flexibility. Each also understands how his or her strengths may be used. Maybe the most important expectation of flexibility is to make clear to the team that even the assumptions about who is good at what will evolve on the depth chart, thereby checking egos.

A SYSTEM REMOVES EGO

Knowing how your team members work together prevents ad hoc, ego-driven decisions. As Kevin, a sales vice president selling human resources services, explained, "If you don't communicate early that team success and cooperation trump even territory, you'll fail at this.

"Egos have to be checked," he continued. "It also has to be worth the individuals' time to cooperate; they're not in this for the charity. If you let everyone run amok, you'll kill accountability and productivity; you have to have a system and some sort of view of everyone who touches sales. But it's important to adjust, because in most complex selling situations, you have numerous buyers with various motives."

Matching the right people with different opportunities worked for Kevin, as he took category sales from $4 million to $17 million in five years.

A Sales Blazer I observed said, "Salespeople are happy to help on anyone's sale if they know it's worth their time, that they will be credited on their input, and they will be helped in return."

Even if you keep your traditional structure, you may flex it on key, strategic accounts. You'll be able to add dimensions to the assignments of each person as long as expectations are set. Start by making the system predictable. Set rules for coordinating primary or overlay assignments to imbed on-the-fly flexibility. Then brainstorm the possible formations for attack. You'll be able to match the talents of your team with any sales opportunity to beat the competition.

THE DEPTH CHART DIFFERENCE

Ordinary salespeople make low complexity the priority instead of maximum area cooperation. Poor managers create a disturbance when they make "their" changes to alignment. Sales Blazers on both levels foresee the need to match talent to opportunity using a flexible but predictable system—a depth chart system. Expert flexibility delivers greater team results, not just territory results.

Play Your Depth Chart is the first of two strategies to effectively engage a team of sales, support, and any expert talent that can help progress to a key close. Fully understanding the many aspects of all parties involved in a sale puts you in a position to connect people in the right way. The result is the ability to create a culture in which everyone is expected to contribute his or her unique strengths to team success using a more flexible, yet predictable, approach. The next chapter presents the second of the strategies that help us *engage* others in our success. *Activate Expectations* helps us understand how to effectively clarify and coordinate assignments to get results.

Strategy Summary—Play Your Depth Chart

1. Set or suggest an expectation of a flexible, team approach that matches the talents of different people to key opportunities.
2. List two or three key prospects on which you and your team can cooperate and invest some time in every day (Chapter 3).
3. Summarize the strengths, talents, motivations, and personality of each team member (Chapter 2).
4. Summarize the strengths, weaknesses, opportunities, and threats of competitors (Chapter 3).
5. Create a depth chart with key prospects, salespeople, and competitors to create the right mix of assignments for strategic efforts.
6. Implement the new system as an overlay to traditional assignments first in order to learn and develop teamwork.

Activate
Expectations

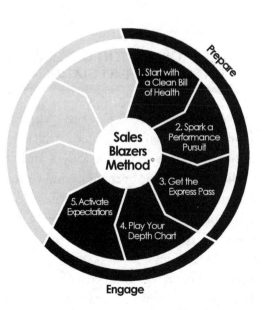

Prepare

1. Start with a Clean Bill of Health

2. Spark a Performance Pursuit

3. Get the Express Pass

4. Play Your Depth Chart

5. Activate Expectations

Sales Blazers Method°

Engage

THE STRATEGY

Set clear expectations and prioritize them to contribute to a sale. Specify a reward for completing each one—*Activate Expectations.*

> *What we will accomplish in this chapter:* We will explain why just setting clear expectations or final goals alone isn't enough. We will review how to define contributions to sales results and connect rewards. We will learn a structure for activating expectations that raises sales performance and then put this strategy in context with the others.

THE PROBLEM: TOO GENERAL, UNTARGETED EXPECTATIONS

A CEO's plan at the beginning of the year would never be stated just as "Grow revenue 25 percent." The board expects specific accomplishments to be stated. Dollar expectations alone are far too general. Yet this is exactly what happens when salespeople talk only in terms of requests and closes. Leading a high-performance team with many different roles takes more than assigning numbers. Pushing accountability is counterproductive unless clear, two-way expectations that really contribute are established along the way.

For example, one team was assigned a quota of $2 million on a complicated product that wasn't ready to ship. With one fact sheet and no experience in selling the product, the team's manager announced the quota publicly to support roles and salespeople with no defined territories. There were no training sessions or individual conversations to define responsibilities. The expectation was simply that the salespeople would figure out how to reach the quota. No one reached it, pay fell, and even key salespeople left before the year was over. The revenue goal was crystal clear, but the work needed to reach it was not.

THE SOLUTION: ACTIVATE EXPECTATIONS

It is important to understand that this chapter is not about the common practice of measuring and rewarding sales activities rather than results—we're not talking about call reports. It's also important to be clear that we are not talking about the obvious importance of rewarding revenue results. We all understand that accountability for final results is fundamental. In observing so many Sales Blazers, there was clearly a third category of rewarded work that was missing in other sales teams—accountability for work that progresses a selling cycle to result, not just achieving the final result. This key strategy was difficult to articulate; however, the Sales Blazers I met with helped pin it down.

Work That Works

This strategy requires describing work specifically and in a way that ensures it really contributes to results. After several failed attempts at losing 30 pounds, for instance, I remember finally figuring out what it really takes to lose weight: a calorie deficit over time (fewer calories taken in than calories used up). The fad-diet industry thrived on me and millions of others, who kept switching among the "expert" spins we heard on late-night TV about various physical activity and desperate 10-day crash diets.

I learned a lesson that many suspect but don't want to accept when I went to a credentialed fitness and nutrition expert.

"The cold, hard truth in weight loss," he said, "is good effort may be better than lack of effort, but effort does not always equal results. Let's get serious and do what it takes. You're going to have to not only do the right things but do them in the right way to create a calorie deficit. It's that simple."

For me, the trainer said a 3,500 weekly calorie deficit would result in a weight loss of 1 pound per week. That is what would really be required if I wanted to lose weight. Anything else might sound like it would work, but it might not result in a enough of a deficit or it might not be sustainable.

A weekly deficit was worth working for because it carried almost no risk. Eating right and exercising correctly seemed harder than the fads but more rewarding, because the weight gradually came off. A consistent weekly deficit to lose a pound a week felt so much more real than a fad that recommended a lot of extra, ineffective activity or a crash diet for results that promised pounds of loss without sustainability. It made me feel that I was doing what was truly required to assure results, and sure enough, the weight came off. Sustainable results are all that matter in weight loss and in sales.

If the sales activities you perform are as general as cold calls, meetings, and proposals, your work is like a fad diet. You may feel like you are doing the right selling activities and have promised results, but your actions are defined too broadly and actually distract from results. Likewise, total focus on quota alone is the crash diet of sales, skipping to one-time results through extreme devices that are virtually impossible to sustain. Weekly achievement of expectations that really contribute to a close is the sales version of creating a healthy deficit and a bal-

ance between calories eaten and calories expended over time—
it efficiently and unavoidably activates sustainable results.

The Third Bucket: Active Expectations

Defining the distinct, common difference between the mag-
netic topics of "accountability" and "activity" was not easy.
Either one could be explored by itself, but Sales Blazers put
expectations and rewards in place that connect the two concepts. These leaders warned that ambiguity truly is death for a
sales leader.

"You have to chunk things down," one said. "You have to keep
tuning what works and hold people accountable for it. Absolutely
everything needs to be clear, accountable, and automatic."

To increase sales, one leader's "key example was clearly
defining how to deal with customers, and then reviewing which
steps needed to be taken and what the outcome would be."

"We must be held accountable, too," said another Sales
Blazer. "You have to reward people more than once a year, and
sometimes that means things other than annual sales goals."

If I had a quarter for every time I heard someone in sales say
"clear expectations," "accountability," or just "results"—well,
you know. Ask some people at any level in sales to go deeper
into any of these topics, and you'll start hearing the same words
about accountability and firing people. The more effective
actions that Sales Blazers expect, however, don't fit into the traditional buckets of "sales activities" or "revenue results."

I had to go back several times to realize that the Sales Blazers
were using a third, seldom seen, "bucket" of sales work. The
third bucket is full of what I call "activated" or "active expectations." This third category, Active Expectations, sounded a

lot like what Kathy and others said that Tony was using as a Midwest regional leader for Sprint.

"He helped us understand that, regardless of how much money we wanted to earn, he would help us identify the exact steps we needed to take to accomplish our goals," one of Tony's people said. "The entire team would work on the exercise, and at the end of the year, those of us who followed this roadmap actually exceeded the expectations we set 12 months earlier."

The result? Tony's team revenue grew nearly 30 percent, while counterparts achieved only 11 percent growth.

Numerous observations showed that there was a common theme of making "specific," "short-term" assignments—active expectations—and "rewarding people for achieving them."

Listening to Sales Blazers, these active expectations they describe are entirely different than simply rewarding "sales activities" or pushing for "results." One salesperson described "verifiable outcomes," others called them "contributions to a close" or "specific assignments in team selling." In some way they all seemed to say, "We find a way to assign and reward things that really do contribute to a sale and a year."

Bo, the Sales Blazer we met in the Introduction, described his challenging year of trying to reach 29 percent growth after ranking number 2 with 18 percent the previous year.

"It took some real soul searching," he said. "It took soul searching to separate what we needed to do, to not look at the mountain—this massive goal; we just needed to take it one step at a time to have any chance at the goal. I had to believe that whatever it looks like right now—if I keep a positive attitude, if we do the things I know are the right things, it will work and I'll accept whatever the outcome is.

"We'd placed some competitive bets early last year," Bo continued. "We broke our strategy down into consumable parts. Everything had to hit. If they didn't all hit in an alignment of the stars, we weren't going to make our number. We had a few things go our way the first half of the year. Sure enough we achieved all that we'd set out to achieve for midway through the year by the smallest of margins."

But because most of Bo's revenue comes at the end of the year, they really weren't halfway up the mountain.

"Now, we looked at all the things we had to do to close the rest of the accounts and make the year," Bo explained. "The team pulled together. We accomplished every consumable part and looked down from the mountain; we ended up at 105 percent of that staggering goal. Like I said, that 105 percent felt bigger than any 150 or 200 percent of goal I'd ever achieved because we broke it down and pulled it all off."

Like Bo's "consumable parts," an active expectation is not one activity micromanaged on a heavy-handed report, it's the important activities described to ensure they contribute directly to a sale.

For example, active expectations are not just cold calls but cold calls that are targeted tightly. They are not just qualified leads but appointments with qualified contacts who have expressed an interest in buying. They aren't support that doesn't really help; they are specific steps of progress, each with multiple characteristics that are really required to close a sale or build a year. They are not proposals e-mailed, but live proposals checked off by prospects' decision makers as complete and fitting. Note that this does not imply that every step in the sales process should become more detailed—this creates make-work. We are talking here about the few critical acts that precede success, whatever those are for a business.

The only thing that remains after completing these active expectations is time, and each expectation has a specific potential reward that helps move things along. In fact, contribution tied to a reward is the motivating combination of activating an expectation.

APPLYING ACTIVE CHARACTERISTICS

It is critical to clarify active expectations from typical sales activities in your mind and in the minds of your colleagues. So, what are the characteristics to add to each activity? It doesn't capture what Sales Blazers do to say, "If we make so many presentations and do so many demos, it will result in this many closes." This is work from the "activity bucket" that might fulfill a mediocre sales goal. But to activate an expectation requires adding specifics to sales activities, such as:

1. Spell out specific criteria that ensure an active expectation *contributes* directly, not indirectly, to a sales result.
2. Ensure that completion is *verifiable*.
3. Define guaranteed, specific *rewards* for each expectation.
4. Offer the appropriate *people* (or positions) the opportunity to achieve various expectations and prioritize them.

Blake Hawkes, a client executive for Advanced Systems Group, Inc., described how activating expectations builds on the previous strategies we have discussed. He said, "I have my best years when I refine my efforts. I look at the process and remove things that aren't essential for me to do personally. If I understand each person on my extended team individually, I can make sure that team members are offered those tasks and can do those tasks within the process which they are very best suited to do. There are those that are virtual team members and those that you could call my 'hard team' members—both part of my depth chart. But in my business there is nothing that progresses a sale more than a face-to-face meeting where the client feels safe in truly telling me where their areas of concern and opportunity in their shop are."

Essentially, Blake described what we learned in our preparation strategies—specifically, to ultimately earn the right to have a trusted Chichen Itza Chat with the decision maker about his or her organization.

Blake's active expectation is this very open meeting of trust with a decision maker—a conversation in which the decision maker feels safe enough to discuss serious challenges that obviously wouldn't be shared with just anyone. For Blake, the characteristics that activate what would otherwise be just a potentially passive sales meeting are having (1) an eye-to-eye conversation with the decision maker, who shares (2) an inside scoop that he or she wouldn't share with just anyone. The sharing of information in person that would never be made public is verifiable; the number of these meetings in a period is measurable.

Blake says, "The reason that this step in our sales process is my priority activity is that if I can get to this point I will absolutely sell something. Measuring how many of these conversations happen is much different than measuring any sales meeting. As far as the people are concerned, to the extent I can specifically refine expectations for the virtual team and make it rewarding for hard team members to take care of as many of the other expectations as they're suited for, I can maximize my time in front of clients to get to this key moment of opening up. Now, the quantity of these meetings is relevant to everyone."

Because active expectations are different for every company and every industry, it is important to craft carefully what your own expectations and activating criteria will look like. The following are some suggestions to start applying active characteristics that you can define more specifically for your business. Look at the activating qualities for each step in a basic sales process, prioritize each, and add your own business specifics to the most important to better ensure contribution, verify completion, specify a reward, and define who can work on which and with what priority.

Examples of Basic Expectations That Might Be Activated for Your Business

Sales 101 Activity	Criteria Needing Customization
Prospecting	Appointment with an authorized decision maker stating interest in buying someone's solution
Sales Support/Meetings	*Opportunity Summary:* A written list of sales opportunities at a prospect, including financial impact, that is agreed to by the decision maker
Proposal	Live presentation to decision maker, with confirmation of the solution's fit, potential, finances, and timing
Transacting/closing	Signed, legal paperwork
Implementation	Signoff by customer on incremental deliverable
Account expansion	A new, reviewed Opportunity Summary, after implementation
Payment receipt	Clearing of payments, not just a purchase order or a check

If you extend active expectations, daily work will offer additional opportunities for everyone, not just tedious assignments.

It will help you and your teammates see the whole plan because everyone understands the parts. Potential energy builds.

With these characteristics in place, you can get a picture of a specific accomplishment and reward—lifted from management's grip—and now within reach. The task and reward are actively waiting for you to grab them.

Initiative that creates results needs to be rewarded more than once a quarter or once a year, much as a calorie deficit should be rewarded every week. The small amount of work it takes to activate and prioritize expectations is worth it. Success breeds success. Why does meaningful success along the way create momentum? Let's take a look.

STRONG BACKING FOR ACTIVATING EXPECTATIONS

How to get more work out of a day has been studied almost as much as anything in business. B. F. Skinner, a famous motivational psychologist, is often cited as an expert on explaining the momentum that clear assignments and rewards can create. We'll quickly cover the basics, but add an important layer from Sales Blazer findings to the science to apply it to people who sell. Let's briefly review the concept.

Skinner showed the power of rewarding actions quite successfully with his ABC model. Skinner's theory can be summarized as something like this: A leader creates an *antecedent*, or prompt, for a desired *behavior*, or expected activity. Natural and secondary *consequences* reinforce the repeated performance of the desired activity.

It may be true that *positive*, *immediate*, and *certain* (PIC) consequences work 17 times better in the lab than *negative immediate consequences* (NIC), but something is missing. The model does not describe the *qualities* of the ABCs that make them relevant to human minds, especially the minds of salespeople. We are not interested in dictating and driving just any behavior. To drive sales results, we need the right prompt, the right activity, the right results, and the right rewards for everyone on the team.

We will cover improving prompts (antecedents) and rewards (consequences) in later chapters. But let's add to Skinner's behavior element by making activities that create results directly more attractive to the people we influence and lead—activate expectations. Experts filling in Skinner's theories found that defining work in small steps and in terms that engage employees in the right work increases performance. Rewarding these tangible steps toward ultimate success also increases performance, and punishment rarely motivates long-term results.

The principle of rewarding small successes is critical, but rewarding small steps that matter is even more important. An active expectation has *verifiable completion* of specific criteria that contribute directly to a sale, and it has its own reward.

Another way to describe setting crystal-clear specifics that really matter is two-way accountability between a leader and those with whom he or she works. Some leaders activate expectations by creating two-way accountability in writing. If the expectations set get done but don't result directly in sales or don't get rewarded, then leaders become accountable to leadership above and to those they attempt to lead. They become accountable to executives for rewarding the wrong things and to colleagues for failing to keep promises for reward.

How do you create accountability on a team that doesn't report to you? The advice to activate expectations is just as powerful for reps who must request action from experts and client committee members and subsequently coordinate progress to close. Clarifying, specifying and describing, possibly in writing, the priority next steps and what the reward will be, as we have discussed, will really move things along. We can even activate expectations to clarify our own work.

Fitting Assignments

Roles are made flexible by varying available assignments. We need to reward active expectations, but it is also important to clarify who gets to do them and what they will gain by doing them. This is especially critical for inviting and getting help from an informal team—like attracting bees with sugar water. Clarifying and communicating requests for specific individuals or roles and specifying the gains to be achieved do wonders. Not only do they reduce overlapping efforts, but they also get the right people doing the right work while allowing them to benefit from doing it. Occasionally, tasks needed to make the area's goal may fall outside a salesperson's territory. Instead of receiving one set of job expectations, each person may be given a different set of expectations. The wrong expectations for the wrong person or the wrong customer waste time.

"Chunking things down" to active expectations works because it creates a better fit for assignments. Performers like to have responsibility for work they are good at. If they see a clear opportunity that is relevant to their skills, they'll usually jump on it. This tendency for sales-related talent to move in the direction of what they're good at should direct salespeople in making requests of others. Leadership should design policies, processes, and assignments so that sales and support people can reach their own expectations and company expectations simultaneously. But whatever the assignments, people must believe the goals are achievable. *Self-efficacy* is often misinterpreted as self-esteem or responsibility. Self-efficacy is really the confidence a person has in his or her ability to perform a specific assignment. It matters to which positions and to which people active expectations are assigned—clarity and confidence create momentum. Experts have also proved that performers carefully scrutinize their work, at least subconsciously, to sense if it is reasonable. Adding the qualities of direct contribution and confidence to what people are asked to do, and then rewarding them upon completion, engages previously lax activity.

Real Expectations

Activating previously soft, broad expectations creates results in two other ways as well. If you are new to sales, it will help you to avoid ambiguity. And if you are more experienced, you expect a professional approach from management to maximize your rewards. No matter what your level, by activating expectations, you are freed from micromanagement of meaningless activity. Activating expectations helps people at all levels thrive in clarity and with a sense of freedom. Sales Blazers use this approach to organize work, avoid team conflict, and increase productivity.

Defining and rewarding active expectations leaves no room for misunderstanding or wasted time—it makes assignments for the last chapter's 30-second change in organization possible. If a flexible organization is the depth-chart half of a team system, then active expectations is the playbook—a complete set of potential, coordinated assignments preloaded to work in different situations. Let's take a look at an example.

Scott, a Sales Blazer, was brought into a technology firm after success at another company leading a struggling team of a dozen salespeople. At the end of the first year, they'd made headway. At the end of the second year, they'd sold 114 percent of goal. I asked Scott and his team about his "whole new model of accountability."

One of Scott's team members repeated the thoughts of many Sales Blazers when he said, "Now everybody is engaged in proactive selling. Everybody has a clear accountability for part of the number." He described how they also have other definite commitments to contribute in specific ways to sales and team goals. Scott talks to team members in various roles and sets up their expectations.

"Everyone, including those we position as non-sales experts, has a commitment sheet every year that includes revenue share, specific contributions, verifiable outcomes, and rewards," the rep said. "Before Scott, things used to be lax and foggy. Support people sat on their hands until someone called them. Sometimes five people would claim the same sale. Salespeople seldom cooperated. Now everyone is clamoring to complete expectations because they matter, to move a deal forward. Support people are calling salespeople to help on opportunities. Salespeople work with each other to reciprocate leads because they'll get something out of it."

"The team was well below its goal, and communication had deteriorated," Scott added. "We made a division between short- and long-term goals. Our specific assignments have measurable outcomes and include things performers are expected to do, supported with commitments by management. We release rewards received for demonstrating the right behavior when the deal closes."

THE PROCESS

Sales Blazers initiate specific team contributions to sales by defining completion and rewards. To do this, create an "Active Expectation Sheet" with each team member that includes available contributions to sales, not just a quota. Include the criteria for each that verifies success and stipulates related rewards. Figure 5.1 shows a general example of a sales process (horizontal arrow and labels), sample active expectations (diagonal arrows), and a reminder to attach some reward (% sign).

Because processes and terms differ for individuals and companies, we won't go through all the details because they may not apply to you. However, let's go through an example of the second step in a sales process determined by its company to be key: "Expanding" and its active expectation, "Opportunities Summary."

The second step in a sales process for this organization requires involving a subject-matter expert, a sales engineer, or

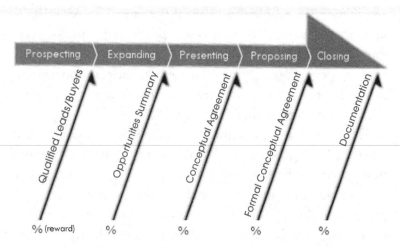

Figure 5.1 Sample Sales Process and Active Expectations

some other specialist to help sell. But, as we learned in the last chapter, a salesperson may also gain leads or expertise from other reps or from specialists outside sales. A company may ask someone with relevant relationships or expertise, regardless of title, to assist the responsible salesperson on a key opportunity.

The idea is to explore all possible ways to "expand" potential revenue within the prospect. For example, a verifiable step in the sales process may allow such an expert to contribute in other territories by writing a summary of all the opportunities in the account—an Opportunities Summary. In this example, completing the Opportunities Summary is the active expectation and has a reward, but there are conditions for completion.

The specialist first has to get permission from the other rep in the opportunity's territory. It's also agreed that a summary isn't complete until all opportunities are detailed, estimated, and deemed realistic by the prospect. (See Figure 5.2.) The rewards attached to the expectation may or may not be enough to sway specialists to add to their own work, but it sets the stage for them to help wherever they can because they will be rewarded. Abundance is required and egos must be checked, but now cooperation makes sense.

Suppose a sales rep seeks a particular skill, even from an outside territory. Another rep with that expertise pursues the chance to help. An Opportunities Summary is written to receive a specific reward; in this illustration to gain a commission as though the outside source had contributed 10 percent of the effort to the sale.

After the summary is validated by the prospect, one of the three opportunities detailed within the account develops into a potential $1,000,000 sale. The summary is calculated to have contributed $100,000 (10 percent) toward team goals, and the

Figure 5.2 Partial Active Expectations

commission of 2 percent of that amount is already in place. A potential $2,000 summary? Self-interest creates an offer to help the sale close, because that is when the reward is given. With team efforts, the deal closes and incentives are given. Mission accomplished.

Another Example from the Field: A Kit, Not Just a Contact

A different example about the first step, prospecting, will help clarify the principle of activating expectations. Robert, a Sales Blazer, sold outsourced sales support. He understands what it takes to create a revenue boost. Robert's team achieved the company high of 130 percent of quota by rewarding proven contributions to sales.

"Getting salespeople to do work that really matters requires thinking outside the box a little bit," explained Robert. "Most of the time, managers just say you need to be sending out so many e-mails a day, making so many cold calls, and making so many live calls a day. I often think that upper management gets caught up in just getting metrics on the board."

Robert explained that most employees, even salespeople, sometimes think that if they're working more than eight hours, even if it's sitting in front of the computer, they're driving results.

"But what are they really getting done?" he asked.

Robert explained that other leaders just keep the ultimate goal in front of sales and support people's faces without really making sure that every day contributes to the annual number.

"What we do is break down impact tasks individually and back into the goal," he described.

Robert said that if they were going to hit their sales goal, they would need to know not only how many customers they needed to present to, but also do a well-thought out, live proposal, not just a written one.

"To get to this point—in front of a CIO (chief information officer)—is pretty tough," Robert admitted. "We found that something called a CIO survival kit was key to getting us in front of the CIO—and sometimes even the CEO—because it had gadgets and messages helpful to a CIO's unique challenges. In that survival kit were some fun things like a handheld computer for the CIO to use to sample our technology, a flashlight and granola bar with a message about our concept to aid surviving as a CIO. So instead of making typical 'drop offs' to the receptionists, we made personal deliveries of survival kits to the CIOs themselves and rewarded them for that."

Robert told a story about a CEO in a corporation who absolutely didn't like his company. He was very engaged with the competition. Through a reseller, the salesperson got a CIO survival kit in front of the CEO and it generated some interest. As a result, they got to speak to the CEO for 15 minutes and built a connection.

"Because of that kit," Robert continued, "we got to make our proposal to both the CIO and CEO and won around $2.5 million of business, all because of thinking out of the normal activity box. If we had just mailed that thing and focused on metrics, we would've posted some meaningless numbers on the board. Or if we had just focused on results, we would not have done the weekly things it took to make the sales goal.

"We simply found the things that really worked and pushed those. We were 130 percent of quota that year."

A Professional Opportunity

Great leaders don't need to be bashful about setting active expectations because they aren't make-work; they are opportunities. Setting active expectations isn't just an edict but a way leaders can help make organizations truly great. Why? Because active expectations ring true, because the specifics make sense, and because rewards are certain.

A great example of this is Beth, a sales rep I've worked with who was recently promoted to vice president. She was promoted not just for her dollar results but because of her ability to lead people. She could get sales and support people focused as a team on the right things for real results. Before her promotion, I spoke to Beth about why others say the people around her "work so well together it's like clockwork." Beth resisted bragging but gave me an example of what I would categorize as activating an expectation.

"Some companies don't have an outbound telesales team," Beth related. "But new qualified leads are the lifeblood of my new business."

What did she do? As she shared with me what she did, I could almost see her presenting a new opportunity to a sales support staffer—the chance to begin to sell, to learn Hoovers, D&B, and other systems—to learn how to develop qualified leads. This opportunity replaced some of what was purely administrative work with ambiguous outcome. Beth gave the staffer the criteria for what could be considered a qualified lead, including employee count, contact type, and a minimum contract potential. Then, she set a verifiable expectation of three to five qualified leads with appointments and tied a small personal bonus to this and other expectations.

One misconception about requests and assignments is that sales and support people hate work and having to work with other people. What they really hate is wasting time, sharing money, and following ambiguous leadership. Predictability of assignments, clarity of leadership, and rewards dialed in appropriately to team members will ramp results and cooperation.

The inspiring observation on this topic was that with the right system of active expectations in play, all types of roles rush to progress a sale. They rush to complete meaningful action that actually contributes to furthering sales opportunities. The right activity increases results when the team knows beforehand how they are to work with each other and what they may be accountable for.

As a great sales leader named Doug said, "You have to track to the most immediate and powerful motivation—results whenever and wherever. Salespeople are impatient; show us results we can achieve right now."

WHERE ACTIVATING EXPECTATIONS FITS

Before activating expectations, it is necessary to understand where you and your team members fit on the depth chart so that you can create a set of potential shifts and assignments and rewards for many situations. Now that we have made our organization more flexible with these middle two strategies, we will learn in the last three chapters how Sales Blazers lead to success.

Strategy Summary—Activate Expectations

1. Set clear, short-term expectations that contribute to a close.
2. Spell out specific criteria that ensure the expectation contributes *directly*, not indirectly, to sales results.
3. Ensure that completion is *verifiable*.
4. Define a guaranteed, specific—even *automated*—reward for completion.
5. If you are a manager, assign which expectations are available for each position and individual on the team and what the priorities are.
6. Put active expectations and rewards in writing every year—on an Active Expectation Sheet.
7. Put the right system in play and all types of roles will clamor to complete meaningful actions that contribute to sales.

Coach Like a Professional

THE STRATEGY

A Sales Blazer is a professional coach—coaching teammates, reps, support staff, or advising client teams. The three coaching advantages Sales Blazers have over others are the right *leader*, *setting*, and *action*. We will explore these three attributes, but simply put, they mean being a respected *leader* who builds a motivational *setting* and demonstrates the best *actions—Coach Like a Professional*.

> *What we will accomplish in this chapter:* We will learn why people refer to Sales Blazers as coaches. We will explore the three characteristics that make an influential coach. We will learn how to create a motivational setting and how to add potency to the actions you request of others.

THE PROBLEM: BLOWING THE BIG THREE

Three things kill the ability of a coach: failing to act like a leader, failing to demonstrate to team members actions that are critical for success, and ruining what could have been a motivational setting. Learning to coach like a professional is really about you as a person, the actions you coach, and the setting you create regardless of the situation.

Like sales coaches, sports coaches win or lose depending on the same three elements: a respected leader, the right actions, and creating the right motivational setting in any situation. Let's look at the problem when one or all of these are missing.

Master motivators don't always yell and hype. They choose the right form of motivation for each situation. Surprisingly, they sometimes quietly highlight the most optimistic but realistic outcome in a situation, and then they intensely renew everyone's focus. They let that renewed focus, not hype, trigger adrenaline. As one ricochet leader said, "There is an important balance here with the 'rah-rah.' 'Rah-rah' without substance is just entertainment."

I came to a realization of my own while observing Sales Blazers: I learned that respect is more linked to action than to talk. I discovered that all the rambling I did early in my career with team members on the way to appointments didn't actually earn much respect. Words alone aren't what salespeople are looking for. They are waiting for a leader who is a great coach whom they can respect. Salespeople notice quickly when a team member or manager just tells them over the phone what they should be doing, asks for activity reports, or rambles in the car after appointments—talk, talk, talk, all talk.

Another mistake is missing the opportunity to create a motivational moment in every situation.

One manager I worked with told me about a senior leader who stalled his own influence with inconsistency. He had a habit of being a "yes man," not only with his boss but also with his subordinates. For example, one of his people discussed with him a new, successful sales channel. The executive congratulated the performer; he encouraged him to continue to pursue the initial success of the channel, and the executive did so in detail. The individual remembered a meeting shortly thereafter with his executive and the CEO.

"The second my executive got a drift of which direction the CEO was going, he jumped off my bandwagon and jumped on the CEO's, even though it completely contradicted his own detailed arguments for the project just hours earlier," he recalls. "He didn't even bring them up. I couldn't believe it. All of a sudden, I had to speak up and give his arguments for him. It was troubling. The sad thing is, this happens all the time."

A leader who is unable to earn respect, demonstrate beneficial actions, or command a situation leaves salespeople with the feeling that nothing gains traction, nothing is real, with their passive leader. Coaches are different—they play leadership roles for everyone involved on both sides of the sale.

THE SOLUTION: COACH LIKE A PROFESSIONAL

The term *teacher* or even *mentor* doesn't fully describe how Sales Blazers help others ramp results. In my research, Sales Blazers were repeatedly referred to as coaches. Observing these great sales leaders more closely reveals that the word *coach* is used so much because these sales leaders are out in the field advising, instructing, motivating, and competing—providing leadership for everyone around them. Clients would call what they experience "advising," but the skill from our side is coaching much more than just talking.

Every other strategy we have discussed involved a lot of effort to articulate clearly the difference between Sales Blazers and mediocre managers. In my research, however, coaching was mentioned and observed so often that it can't really be called a metaphor. The fact is that salespeople who achieve extraordinary results with a group *are* coaches, who are paid to coach with professional skill.

One Sales Blazer named Doug, with whom I worked closely, was a model of honorable behavior and disciplined demonstration. Doug's counterparts achieved 3 percent growth, while he ranked number 1 among sales leaders. It was impossible, as a colleague or a prospect, not to respect Doug. His disciplined character was apparent. His habit of persistently communicating best practices from other clients, parts of the field, and headquarters made him easy to follow. He habitually spoke the most encouraging words and provided vision within accounts. We have all had a "Doug" in our career, a person we remember as honorable, who works hard to demonstrate what the company can offer, and who creates a discipline of motivation.

In Chapter 2 we discussed findings that show we can improve the quality and persistence of performance if we design work according to a process of *internalization*. Behavioral expert Herbert Kelman, who developed this model of influence, includes another dimension (see Figure 6.1). This second dimension increases the likelihood that a performer will respond to a leader's request for an action.

Leaders send messages intentionally or unintentionally in the three ways we have discussed. They don't just teach with words; they send messages as well by being who they are (*leader*). Leaders motivate in motivational sales settings (*setting*), and they demonstrate actions and their benefits to those they lead in the process, not just the customer (*actions*).

First, the type of person you are matters. Coaches have the opportunity to get close enough to team members to earn their high respect. This high respect is honor, earned only through

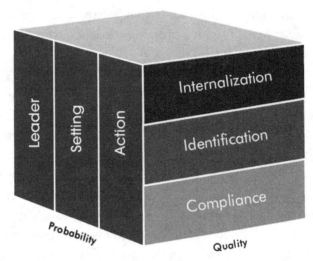

Figure 6.1 Kelman's Model of Influence

honesty, fairness, and integrity. It is earned before it is asked for, and it distinguishes these leaders from others. Influential coaches gain this high respect by showing the power *and* inclination to champion what salespeople are trying to get done. In his model, Kelman explains that mediocre managers damage their influence with workers by being "detrimental to the achievement of goals."

As Kelman found, long-term influence does not come from just being liked. And influence is damaged by being "publicly identified with illegal or socially disapproved activities." News stories of bribery, fraud, or the offering of inappropriate favors in sales situations reveal some of the extreme, obvious examples of dishonor. In contrast, the belief of great coaches in the business purpose and in mutual respect enhances their ability to influence others over the long term.

Second, coaches also get out and create a motivational setting in the field in any situation. We will see excellent examples of these later, but they gain advantage in boosting others' performance that only a motivational setting can bring.

Third, great coaches create *prepotency*, making the doing of the action attractive to their team members. They do this by making the action appeal to others as the most personally relevant and beneficial option for how to spend their time. They also demonstrate the action with superior knowledge, by example, and by selling the benefit of the action.

What Does Great Coaching Look Like?

In the example that follows, see if you can pick out the three qualities of coaching that we have been discussing: being a respected *leader*, demonstrating the right *action*, and creating the right motivational *setting*.

It was apparent from their comments that one inspirational Sales Blazer named Scott had the respect of those with whom he worked. I asked Scott for an example of coaching.

"We sell software, and at one time were trying to displace a competitor at a telecommunications company," he began. "We needed one of our divisions to partner with our prospect. The salesperson on the account was a veteran but was new to telecomm. The salesperson had discussion after discussion with our sister division about the company's opportunity, and he hit roadblock after roadblock.

"Finally, we were doing some prep work, and I said, 'I know you may not think a less direct approach is what we ought to take, but please just trust me once and see what comes of a less direct approach.' I went on one of his calls, and we made progress within 10 minutes. It wasn't me; it was the approach."

Scott had a respected reputation in the division, and it was the opportunity to demonstrate the approach he was taking that made the difference. He would say to the division's leaders, "Look, help me understand what things you think are good and bad about this potential partnership. Why doesn't it excite you?" Scott stopped selling corporate gain and started problem solving on a more personal level. He would go through the process of connecting with these people and focus entirely on their opportunity.

Scott remembered, "I would follow up with a question like: 'What if we could do this option that would completely avoid the bad and help you make your department's budget easily this year?' All of a sudden the roadblocks started coming down. At first my rep couldn't believe it; he didn't understand it. My rep could not believe the outcome. But it wasn't going to work for me to try to do the whole deal, so I had to do some quick coaching.

"I said, 'Next meeting, you've got to do a little genuine dancing and talk so these people feel heard and can focus on what they gain. These are our own internal people who don't think they have a problem we can solve and therefore don't need to help us. Keep asking what they are after. Then, we have to deliver.'"

The salesperson had been selling like a pro, but it wasn't the kind of action the division needed, and e-mail from a teammate wasn't going to change anything. Coaches know what to do at the right time and demonstrate it in the field.

"They saw the salesperson as a bull in a china shop," Scott continued. "He needed coaching; he needed to see and hear the conversations take place and see the approach work. He needed to see the people being asked to move outside of the box, then move for us because we were problem solving, not pushing. He also needed to be reminded how he would benefit.

"It was critical to go with him both to the customer and to the internal customers to demonstrate the approach from start to finish. His approach wasn't wrong; it was a textbook direct approach, but it needed to get to a more advanced consultative level. He was a pro and adapted immediately."

The steps Scott and this salesperson were taking and the potential benefits quickly went up through the organization for approvals. The client was now also being influenced in an indirect approach, seeing benefits as the others would like to see them. Scott's tone always carried a degree of modesty, and I gained tremendous respect for him as we worked together. His counterparts never would have listened to a leader they didn't respect. The rep never could have done it alone, not without seeing exactly what to do in the field in a real setting. We all need a coach in certain moments, and only pride can get in our way.

As Scott said, "Then, he was able to do it better than the coach. That's what coaching is all about."

Even skilled veterans like Scott's teammate, who claim they want to be left alone, want coaching, but they want it only when it's needed. Coaching may be needed to demonstrate new products, new policies, or a new type of contact. Because truly great salespeople listen and have some humility, they find coaching helpful in new situations, but they don't stop being leaders themselves. Great salespeople expect a coach not only to have the power to effect change but also to have honor, ability, and the skill to motivate respectfully.

Seeing yourself as a coach requires a much higher standard than that of just a sales rep or even a sales manager. It implies value that someone who is merely working a process doesn't bring. You see and hear this with salespeople who say, "He is always such a positive coach," "She acts as an effective coach and motivator," or "He has a real coaching philosophy."

Characteristics of a great sales leader as described by many salespeople included "one-on-one coaching," "energy, passion, and coaching," and "coach me into my strengths, don't always try to correct my weaknesses." This is so important. All salespeople need to be comfortable in their "skin." Focusing too much on weaknesses will undermine confidence and, ultimately, results.

Some of the prerequisites mentioned for becoming a great coach include "establish other coaches for particular skills on the team," "coach every single day," and "rally the team." An important insight from one rep was that for coaches and reps to be successful, "they have to be open to coaching in the first place."

What do these observations about coaching show? Simply this: Effective sales leaders exude the countenance and expertise of a professional coach. Let's take a closer look at each of the three coaching attributes individually.

FIRST ATTRIBUTE: THE HONORABLE LEADER

How do Sales Blazers, successful sports coaches, and great historical leaders carry themselves? With honor. Remember that honor is a high respect that creates natural distinction. For example, in his noted work, *1776*, author David McCullough describes George Washington as one of the greatest leaders in history.

"He carried himself like a soldier and sat a horse like a perfect Virginia gentleman," writes McCullough. "It was the look and bearing of a man accustomed to respect and to being obeyed. He was not austere. There was no hint of arrogance. 'Amiable' and 'modest' were words frequently used to describe him, and there was a softness in his eyes that people remembered. Yet he had a certain distance in manner that set him off from, or above, others. 'Be easy . . . but not too familiar,' he advised his officers, 'Lest you subject yourself to a want of that respect, which is necessary to support a proper command.'"

McCullough describes how the Philadelphia physician and patriot, Benjamin Rush, a staunch admirer, recorded that Washington "has so much martial dignity in his deportment that you would distinguish him to be a general and a soldier from among 10,000 people. There is not a king in Europe that would not look like a *valet de chambre* [personal attendant] by his side."

Washington's effect on his troops and young officers was unparalleled. As Rush recorded, "Joy was visible on every countenance and it seemed as if the spirit of conquest breathed through the whole army."

It's reaffirming that descriptions of George Washington echo Kelman's model and observations of successful sports coaches. All three possessed the same honorable attributes as Sales Blazers. The fact that honorable coaching makes a person a better leader is well grounded.

Perspective Earns Respect

The coaches I have observed who are very successful don't constantly try to prove themselves but really work to keep perspective—to keep the program grounded and focused. They elevate their own game, but they stay the same humble people.

For example, Mark Panella of the De La Salle coaching staff, whom we met in Chapter 4, said, "If you saw our head coach walking down the street in this town, you wouldn't even recognize him, but the players sure would."

As we noted earlier, Bob Ladouceur is the person who would normally be considered the head coach and one of the most successful coaches in history.

"Bob gains respect because he doesn't try to stick out," Mark continued. "There's humility in the program. For example, we as coaches don't have titles. None of us care if we get any accolades; it's about the kids' success."

As Mark pointed out, coaches with far less success are usually celebrities in their own communities, but they are not always respected as people. There's also a big difference between honor's high respect and the approach you see sometimes in Little League athletics. Amateur coaches often take the focus off the sport and off the kids and put it on themselves, losing respect as they demean and scream at 10-year-olds. In successful programs it is not about the coach, but about the team's task. It's about coaching like a professional.

Mark Zierott, a Sales Blazer at National City Home Mortgage, is respected for his team perspective.

"He is one of the top managers in the company because it's not about him; it's about the salespeople and the team," one of his salespeople said. "And it's not about him winning today; it's about maximizing everyone's opportunity over time. He couldn't care less about getting the accolades."

A team member of a Sales Blazer named Dave underscored how strong humility builds respect.

"Area revenue was growing at a rate of 5 percent. Not only did Dave increase revenue to a rate of 15–20 percent, but he also maintains a focus," she said. "It is more of a coaching philosophy; employees feel more on par with the leader rather than having strictly a boss–employee relationship. Dave holds high expectations and believes strongly in empowerment; he's always looking for ways employees can succeed on their own, ways they can figure it out rather than having to be told what to do."

The rep described how Dave motivated constantly with "excitement and energy" instead of criticism and threats, and emphasized that he also gained great respect through a "service-oriented approach."

Does gaining high respect or honor take a long time? A few months ago, I listened in on a conference call with a sales rep named Debbie, whom I had never met. She was in Boston, the client was in Italy, and I was with another consultant in the West. Debbie was supposed to be selling merchandise, but the client had more urgent needs about sales and service that weren't even related. This rep was excited about her new company, so we expected enthusiasm, but what we heard next amazed both of us: Debbie was *listening*. Without trying to sell things, she began advising the client on creative services, consulting services, and results that she'd seen that were related to customer experience. I literally hit the mute button four times to say to the other consultant, "Can you believe this? It sounds like she's been selling here for years." Why? Because she was coaching, and it wasn't even about her core products. Of course, the client ended up buying $140,000 of those products soon after. Perhaps most amazing to me was that I'd witnessed a similar coaching experience in a meeting with Dianne, the rep in the next territory. Two amazing coaches in the same area? I had to ask Debbie about their manager's coaching.

"Doug is an amazing coach," Debbie said. "Doug is the perfect person to bounce ideas off, but he also assumes success. What I mean is that clients and I don't ever feel like we have to convince him we should move in a certain direction on an opportunity. When consulting with customers, he comes in and starts working, fully believing that the client, with our help, can work to be where they need to be. That is not to say that he does not challenge an idea; he is the first one to question the 'why' of a direction, but he actively listens to the response."

Debbie shared with me that Doug will occasionally suggest fully changing direction on an opportunity, but it is not a battle of wills. The conversation is completely open, with everyone involved.

"For Doug," Debbie continued, "the goal is always to identify the 'right thing to do,' a phrase you frequently hear from him. As the direction becomes clear, he makes you feel confident by encouraging you, removing obstacles, and getting the resources needed for success. He does these things to such a degree that he is different than any other coach I've had, more than supposed sales mentors in the past. I so respect the underlying sense of support, teamwork, and dedication he has. And most of all he walks his talk—if he says something, he does it."

I had talked to Dianne, Doug's other rep, about him too. She had also told me that when he shares his thoughts, they come from experience and expertise. People just want to listen to Doug. She had mentioned repeatedly his respect for people, which had earned her respect for him not just as a manager or salesperson, but as a person.

Finally, I asked Doug about his coaching philosophy. He responded humbly, as you'd suspect.

"I really try to remember that all the people that I work with are people," Doug said. "All of us deserve to be treated with dignity and respect. I really try to treat people how I think they would like me to treat them."

I asked Doug how to gain a client's respect. He emphasized that with salespeople, support people, and clients, it is critical to be proactive rather than reactive.

"Being a coach really is a race to help the customer," Doug continued, "to even help them understand what their true needs might be. The key to sustaining client programs is to not just keep the services up to date. The key to coaching is to recommend and ensure solutions proactively that will help clients achieve their objectives rather than reacting to things that they may be looking for—something that we may have."

Doug's team is like a coaching staff, and they demonstrated as a team that you can earn respect quickly.

Competitive Teamwork Creates Honor

Engaging with others in healthy competitiveness can create a sense of teamwork and honor. Salespeople consistently reported great respect for leaders' "attentiveness, selling skills, and character." Salespeople spoke of respecting leaders who helped develop "revenue that was previously untapped, and each sale was new revenue, always from competitors and at their expense." Salespeople expressed respect for coaching during competitive situations. One person said, "She acts as an effective coach and motivator and provides constructive feedback. She respects and supports the team. Respect is an essential part of the department and she goes to bat for us, facilitating through challenges."

Finally, salespeople say that leaders who put themselves "on the line" for the sake of the team gain high respect and earn honor. RC, a Sales Blazer in commercial real estate, is an example. He impressively skyrocketed revenue and made partner. RC clarified the kind of confidence a team must feel in their leader.

"Leaders have to be respected as coaches," he said. "The team has to look to you as the one who usually provides the resources for a solution, and if you have the confidence the job can be done, it will be done. As a leader, you must be prepared to put yourself on the line and be the one to lead the team to success. This doesn't mean you do everything. You have to achieve success with your team and through your team. If you aren't able to do that, you don't get to be leader anymore. The ultimate success of the deal or the goal comes as a result of being near the game and coaching the team in the field to success."

Kelman's leader, an influencing "agent": What a leader asks of a team member is, deliberately or not, compared to the leader's characteristics: for example, her prestige, status, special knowledge or expertise, group membership, control of certain resources, or ability to apply sanction. It's more likely that people will honor a leader's power if they believe the leader will in fact use the resources available to help people. In other words, using power to benefit is true power; just having potential power is not. People will perform if they recognize true power.

SECOND ATTRIBUTE: MOTIVATE IN
ANY SETTING AND SITUATION

There are as many ways to create a motivational setting as there are situations. The best coaches offer a surprising perspective about creating a motivational setting. Rather than describing pep rallies, screaming, or a high-pressure sales pitch, they find a different motivation for each moment. Motivation isn't always yelling and hype.

For instance, if you visit some campuses with top athletic programs, you might not even be able to see signs of a nationally ranked team. For championship coaches, academics and the school—even the fight song—are important to the team. In the case of De La Salle's winning streak, they thrived on perspective rather than hype. They focused on where performers needed to stay mentally.

"We don't display banners or anything about athletics around campus," said Mark. "We keep athletics where it belongs—inside the gym and on the field. We've got banners hanging there, and right off the gym is a little trophy case. On the field and in the locker room is where the motivation and intensity happen. In our situation, we need to maintain the kids' focus. Our challenge is to keep 15-, 16-, and 17-year-old kids motivated and focused in very different situations. It's not easy. You have to gain their attention and work at it."

Ultrasuccessful coaches are in a unique situation. But isn't every situation in life unique? Some coaches like cookie-cutter pep rallies a little more—which, if they work, are exactly what they should use. But successful coaches describe a more varied approach that allows for different situations. Clearly, successful coaches create an atmosphere of focus that is right for each situation. In one situation, creating an understated environment of focus may be right; in another it will miss the mark.

Consider this example of creating the right setting. I walked into a sales office in Cincinnati that was painted in bright colors. I asked what the new paint job was all about.

"We sell here. You've got to put a place together where people can perform," the regional manager said. "When I got here, it looked like a typical cluttered office. We couldn't stay upbeat. Distraction from sitting in the middle of scrap adds up during the day. There's a lot of rejection that happens here. I decided things better be bright and light to keep people bouncing back."

Another way a great coach can create a selling environment just before a tough presentation, whether in the office setting or in the lobby, is to create a mindset.

For example, RC said, "I am absolutely, always positive. In this business, lackluster results present the end of a career. It is my job to never stop believing there is a realistic solution in any situation. I never find myself accepting a dead end because, as coach, it stops the process.

"Team members thrive when the leader rejects a negative thought process and transitions to the optimum solution," he continued. "That is a positive feeling. When you finish a call, for example, it has to be clear to everybody involved that there is a positive base of solutions, no question. For the team to keep seeing solutions, they definitely have to feel like I'm up."

Joe, who recently received a promotion for his performance, shared his insights on stepping up as a leader to motivate teammates just before his promotion.

"If you find yourself in a situation where you're leading people through a long or complex sales cycle," Joe said, "you can't micromanage. Don't question teammates about things that don't directly relate to necessary steps toward the goal. For example, if someone is walking out the door with golf clubs, don't ask where they're going. Don't ask about generic call reports, ask about the successes."

Joe emphasized the need to keep real, personal opportunities in front of people so they can see and even taste them. He spoke about the importance of being the one to support clients or teammates with confidence, because sometimes they just need to hear that it is really going to happen. Earn the trust of everyone you work with, and motivate them by noticing and recognizing successes.

THIRD ATTRIBUTE: DEMONSTRATING BENEFICIAL ACTIONS

Setting and action together: Sales Blazers are excellent at field demonstration; mediocre salespeople offer unwarranted feedback, mostly in the office. Mediocre salespeople teach product benefits for clients; Sales Blazers illuminate benefits to each person involved in the buying and selling—individual and team benefits of doing business effectively in a particular way.

The third critical element as a coach is demonstrating the right action at the right time. Then, sell the benefits to each client contact and team member. A more reactive instruction, feedback, is covered in the next chapter, but proactively advising and motivating in the field is critical. For example, product knowledge is fundamental, but product knowledge alone does not amount to coaching capability.

As one leader said, "Product knowledge is critical but expected. Many poor performers actually hide behind their product knowledge. Product knowledge alone is not leadership."

Successful leaders teach ability in the field; they don't just communicate knowledge. Sales Blazers change the direction of performance by coaching in the field, gaining a demonstration opportunity that their own office doesn't offer.

The Real Thing

Another area of coaching that a salesperson used to highlight the importance of demonstrating actions in live settings is voice coaching. The details of her example are a much better illustration of how a coach can work with a salesperson than a scene of a manager rambling on in an office.

Voice coaching is not sitting in a junior high school choir class with a teacher up in front of the classroom. No respectable voice coach let's you sit during a lesson. Instead, you stand straight, alone and eye to eye with the voice coach.

The coach listens intently to your use of intonation. At the same time, the coach leads you through the measures precisely. When the moment comes for that high note, she may lift you above your note by demonstrating herself. As she sings, she coaches you to lift the back of your palate, using a visual cue. She arches the hand she's been leading with and gently pulls up on her lips with the other hand until the back of her throat lifts—and yours does too. She stands close, so her example is unmistakable and the leading gently assertive. If you don't get it right the first time, she'll have you start again from the very beginning—and again and again until you get it right. That's why they call her a voice coach and not a teacher—she's a partner in demonstrating action and preparing performers for the stage. Great sales coaches do the same for upcoming sales performances.

"D for . . . 3-D"

I learned something fascinating about live drills from talking to various coaches—a three-dimensional nuance that applies to new reps entering the field. Professional athletic coaches say that players have always learned using playbooks, but a few years ago things changed. Coaches were, almost at once, surprised that many of their young performers learned differently. Just 10 years ago, athletes and others spent a lot of time in classrooms, staring at the chalkboard—"Here's the X, here's the O, here's where you move . . . here's how you add, here's how you sell, here's how you buy."

Today's generation, however, are not linear learners; they are *experiential* learners—three-dimensional learners. They learn football playing 3D video games long before they get their first youth league playbook (just as many young singers now learn how to lift their palates by watching the pros do it on a phone screen). Sales reps learn to sell and buyers to buy, and both learn to cooperate on the Web as children before they enter the workforce. It's all experiential, real-time, visual—three-dimensional.

We need to take this new awareness about performers' learning and incorporate it into our demonstration of the right action. We need to get our players out in the field and demonstrate, and use video files more than using linear dialogue or drawing Xs and Os on a chalkboard. We need to get close, right in the middle of things—even if it's in the middle of a sleet storm—and say, "Here's what you're doing, here's what you need to do, and here's how it will benefit you." We'll do this so they will understand what they are doing well and what they are not doing at all. The more ways you can find to show people experientially how to do the right thing, the more quickly they will learn how to do it.

Tina's salespeople, for instance, expect their coach to demonstrate in three-dimensional ways. Tina is a respected leader and coach whose team has stayed in the top 10 percent for growth at Avon for several years, and this year, her team ranked first. She formally instructs something called a product-and-skill update every week, and she also demonstrates skills and benefits nearly every day in the field. She not only instructs salespeople how to use the actual products, she also inspires both them and their clients with the personal benefit of successfully performing the action just so. She actually demonstrates how the salesperson can counter price competition and get the client to focus on more important issues in every situation.

Bryan, who received a promotion for his performance last year, commented on succeeding by being perceived as an advisor to clients about what to do next.

"I refuse to be seen as just a salesman, I try to be perceived as an advisor who gets paid by providing programs that accelerate performance. This makes negotiating price less necessary."

I observed meetings with Bryan in which his whole demonstration was about the actions that would help the client benefit at a high level.

In a consultative, team situation, practice and role-playing provide one method. Sales Blazers recognize that some people, especially nonsalespeople, have allergic reactions to formal role-playing. These Sales Blazers find a way around this; after each situation, they ask, "How would you say it?" and offer constructive feedback or get others to build on the demonstration. This kind of iterative approach can only be described as coaching, not what we generally understand as teaching or managing.

RC, the real estate leader, highlighted the dimension of timing that makes field demonstration so critical.

"Demonstration in the field is critical to learn timing," he said. "You have to get in the field to show people by example how it is you want them to do the job you're asking them to do in the actual situation; that's what training as a coach is about. The field has some advantages because most of the actions we take in life have to do with timing. Book or classroom-style learning doesn't give you any sense of timing. Experience gives you a sense of timing—when you're talking to people, when you're negotiating with people, and ultimately, when you're performing for people. Timing is the key, and a book doesn't teach you about timing."

Benefits of the Right Action

The most beneficial demonstration associates language about timing and benefits to a performer with an action. Making the action itself attractive is key. I asked Coach Mark about raising the level of an athlete's effort and thought process during drills on the field. He reiterated the importance of demonstration, visual feedback, and repetition. But he also talked about how you can better communicate the results and benefits to the player while demonstrating those things physically.

"Out in the field," Mark said, "we challenge them to dig down deep inside to bring out their absolute best, and we give them a vision of the results if they do. We describe the success so they can visualize it. We're perfectionists; we're going to run the play until they get it right—until they catch the vision and do it right. If we don't get it right, we're not going to leave the field until we do. We are constantly thinking, 'How can I challenge him to see what is possible—how to be a better player than he is?' You stay positive when you have to get on them, 'I've seen you run so much harder. You're not running hard, you are so fast. You can do this!'"

Imagine the skill level of sales teams if we trained and demanded the same degree of vision and perfection from each other around selling new products. You may say, "You'll really want to do it this way because this and that will happen for you." Occasionally, you may have to say, "Hey, you're going down the wrong path, you can gain more a different way. What about this way?" Our job is to help team members to do their best. We can't just focus on our urgencies; like coaches, we have to make the important actions attractive and connect the benefits to the worlds of the team members. As a Sales Blazer, you can make this a reality—"You can do this!"

Multidimensional and Full-Circle

For Sales Blazers, coaching isn't just about technique or next steps, and it goes beyond getting out of the classroom or office. Successful coaches in all areas said things that harmonize with the other leadership strategies.

"You can try to make motivating players a science, but it's tough because the athletes do things that are so unpredictable," said one coach. This leader and others also said that it's not just opportunities that change; performers' lives change. They're not static Xs and Os on an organizational chart.

We are leaders of people first, and process managers second. We concern ourselves with nearly everything about colleagues and find out how to offer them reasons to work a little bit harder—"to get the assignment right."

As Mark said, "For players, there are things that go on every single day at school and at home that we try to bring to light. You've got to find each player and challenge yourself to find out what makes this one tick. We're concerned about their schoolwork, home, their family life, and even their mom— what's going on. We drill into the players' heads that we're concerned about all the guys all day—that effort and focus they give on the field is an extension of that ability everywhere else."

Demonstrating a technique's personal benefit to an expert salesperson's income and to a client's life is important, too. I asked RC if he thought coaching was important for veterans on both sides. He explained that the ability to coach veterans in any role requires that you bring your influence full-circle— right back to understanding who the person is becoming and aligning this with the situation he or she is in.

"If you are trying to maintain leadership with experienced people," he explained, "then yes, selling what needs to be done, how to do it, and what they'll gain is still key. That means that you have to stay ahead of the game, you have to be the one who ultimately has the skill set for leadership. A rep or client advocate can be your best salesperson, but if you are not bringing more to the table than they bring alone, you won't get to be leader. The extra expertise you bring has to be communicated to the person you're leading in a natural, positive way.

You have to bring benefit. The best setting to do that is out in the field, not back home in a meeting."

RC explained that the field is where results happen. Great sales coaches command respect in the field and demonstrate actions proficiently. Sales Blazers coach like a professional.

THE PROCESS: IS THERE A STEP-BY-STEP PATTERN?

So what is the step-by-step pattern? Becoming a great coach might be the most obvious differentiator of a successful sales leader, but it might also be the hardest to achieve. A good place to start is to make yourself deserving of respect. The clear message of Sales Blazers is not to recommend or do anything with or in front of your team members that could be seen by anyone as dishonorable, even if it is popular on your team. Any positive results of dishonorable behavior will be short-lived. While you are becoming that leader who is even more deserving of high respect and power, get out in the field and demonstrate the vision of what should be done, and energize your people with what will be gained. It is also critical to coach clients tactfully as well.

One Sales Blazer named Gail, who leads cross-functional teams on large national accounts, noted how important coaching can be to clients too. "Coaching is critical in leading cross-functional teams in a sales cycle, but we've won major deals with name-brand accounts by sharing our philosophy and practices on coaching," she said.

Sales Blazers create motivational settings and situations in which their team members can respect them. Then they demonstrate skillfully. With a stake in finances and in people, coaches hide less behind paperwork and become active in the field to encourage others to perform precisely the tasks needed to benefit them the most.

All eight strategies are leadership strategies, not watered down for all business situations, but focused specifically for the sales context. The last three strategies of the Sales Blazer Method focus on the actual act of leading the charge after preparing and engaging a team to succeed. In the next chapter, we will look more closely at the all-important feedback that coaches are expected to give as they lead. Remember that, in every situation, Sales Blazers coach and inspire so that the people around them can see possibilities to engage rather than to retreat. "Go, fight, win!"

Strategy Summary—Coach Like a Professional

1. Deserve the honor of a *leader* who brings out the best in people; don't just be a manager with a tough style or a popular personality.
2. Coach by creating motivational *settings* in any situation, settings in which your teammates and clients can visualize performance, focus, and be inspired.
3. Get away from the chalkboard and out in the field. Use the dimensions of reality to demonstrate *actions*—the clear and obvious difference in great and poor coaching styles.
4. Create a vision for team members on both sides of how they will personally benefit from succeeding in a particular situation. This is the most important part of demonstrating an action.

RSVP Feedback

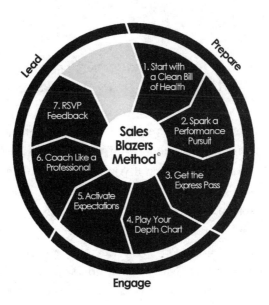

THE STRATEGY

Redirect those you lead with frequent, encouraging feedback that is instructive and invites a pledge for follow-up—*RSVP Feedback.*

> *What we will accomplish in this chapter:* We will explore the damage to progress that the wrong kind of feedback can create. We will examine when feedback should be given, when it should be positive, and when it should be negative. We will gain an understanding of what RSVP feedback is so you can make your constructive feedback most effective.

THE PROBLEM: THE WRONG FEEDBACK HURTS MORE THAN IT HELPS

In a consultative selling situation you have to lead people who don't work for you all the time—clients, contacts, support people, accountants, influencers in the prospect, other members of your sales team. Even if you are not a manager, to lead to success as a Sales Blazer you must provide others with the right feedback to achieve higher revenue goals.

Most people are starved for positive, useful feedback. However, a rambling sales pro with misperceptions frustrates anyone he's working with and hinders performance. And, whether you are a manager or a rep, if you don't offer fair, helpful feedback, you can create a negative financial impact.

Thick-Skinned or Thick-Headed?

Thick skin is needed in sales. Salespeople must sometimes survive hasty, ill-conceived critiques on how an account was handled or on results. The ability to give constructive feedback is the leadership attribute of Sales Blazers that correlates most with sales growth.

Leading with the correct feedback must be taken seriously because it touches so many points of performance, as we will see. But are there times when feedback hurts results?

"If it is said in the wrong way," one leader explained, "or at the wrong time, one misstatement can hurt an individual's focus for years, regardless of its validity."

I thought back to my first week of fifth grade. I was asked by my advanced-math teacher to do a long-division problem on the board while she left for a minute. When she came back, I was still stumped. My fourth-grade teacher had taught us a different method, and the other kids confused me as they shouted instructions. Even though my former classmates and I were in a completely new situation and were expected to perform new math, the teacher went right after me.

"You can't do this?" she asked, surprised. "If you can't even do division, you're not ready for my class. I'll be right back, class. I'm taking Mark to basic math. Keep quiet."

> *Warning:* Mediocre sales reps and managers are comforted by the sound of their own voices and often merely talk to avoid the work that valuable feedback takes.

As often happens with aggressive leaders, no one dared question my teacher's timing or approach. She chose convenience instead of using the moment to build results. It wasn't just my performance that suffered; my former classmates remained and suffered. It took me years to regain my math focus. What a waste of time and performance lousy feedback causes. In contrast, the right kind of feedback improves the performance process and creates growth.

THE SOLUTION: THREE FEEDBACK PHASES, INCLUDING AN RSVP

Mediocre salespeople usually fight more of a battle to boost the amount of effort rather than the quality of effort. Sales Blazers encourage both. They offer guidance that redirects individuals they must lead to work efforts that really move a sale instead of tasks that only sound like selling (see Chapter 5: "Activate Expectations"). Sometimes a short comment is all that is needed, if it's the right recommendation glowing with the right intent.

Scores of sales and support people who gained from the impact of feedback that Sales Blazers provided said things such as "His feedback is what I value most" or "His feedback is an art form; you never feel criticized." They emphasized that they valued "honesty," "clear communication about needed change," "clear and frequent communications without micromanaging," and good, "two-way communication."

Salespeople gained more by making adjustments toward their strengths rather than trying to completely reconstruct an outright weakness. Salespeople also noted that even positive feedback can be offered in the wrong way. Sometimes leaders need to stop the sweet talk and just provide a blueprint for change.

Flattery is not what Sales Blazers use to redirect people's results. Feedback is clearly more important than just a way to motivate. The right feedback at the right time gets people—both internally and externally—moving in the right direction and raises the probability of results.

Sales Blazers intuitively go through three quick steps to give feedback with impact. We'll explore each one of the following:

1. *Bite your tongue or let it rip.*
   Decide whether to give feedback at all.

2. *Use the mental-error concept.*
   Choose between constructive and negative feedback.

3. *Offer the RSVP style of feedback.*
   Embed follow-up in your feedback.

STEP 1: BITE YOUR TONGUE OR LET IT RIP

One Sales Blazer I observed, Kelly, built company sales to millions quickly. He built a team of 140 employees and guided the company he founded, Center7, to successful growth. He attributes much of his leadership success to feedback. I discovered quickly that he has made himself a master of giving feedback. Offering feedback to so many salespeople and technology engineers required Kelly to make a science of offering the right words in environments where pocketbooks and strongly held technology persuasions are at stake. His advice really echoed the importance so many great leaders place on crafting feedback and doing so in a remarkably coherent way.

"I want to actually add value by giving feedback," Kelly said. "First, I decide if I should even say something. This first step, a self-censorship or editing, involves asking yourself four questions:

First, Is what I am about to offer valuable?
Second, Do they deserve it?
Third, Will they receive—or accept—the feedback?
Fourth, Am I too focused on being nice?"

First Question: Is It Valuable?

"First question: Do you have anything valuable to offer? You'd better really think about that," Kelly said. "I don't start babbling about something that I think is wrong or spew catch phrases like save money, work harder, and be nice to others. I must have something deeper and more insightful to offer. This means I have to pay attention to and be more attuned to the individual I hope to invest feedback in."

In some cases, early correction holds amazing value. One leader clarified that he imagines he would be a better chess player if someone had been there to prevent him from learning bad habits. Instead, he played with people who were not much better than he was. Their feedback was just too simple—to remind him to think ahead and a few other basic pointers.

"I make sure I have something more specific to offer," Kelly agreed. "I might take notes in meetings about how a person could change the approach, the process, or some technique; it has to be specific to that person and that situation and not too broad."

A big advantage Sales Blazers find in first considering what they have to offer is that it puts them in touch with the value of the feedback from the receiver's perspective.

A Sales Blazer named Spencer in business-to-business office supplies had a former coworker who didn't ask, "Is my feedback valuable?" About every six months, the coworker would just come up and matter-of-factly say, "Did you know you have a zit on your nose?"

"No. I didn't see this giant thing when I combed my hair this morning," Spencer would think.

Sales Blazers see feedback as something "I have but it's really not mine, at least it does not do me much good if I keep it, and it may have tremendous value for the recipient."

"There is nothing I like to give away more than something that has great value to the recipient and none to me," Kelly explained. "It still takes effort to invest in it though. If you have this concept in your heart when you deliver feedback, it sets you up for a positive experience."

> *Feedback is a valuable investment:* Great leaders understand that feedback is an investment in someone who deserves it; it's a duty owed to the recipient.

Second Question: Do They Deserve It?

Sometimes a salesperson has had the wrong mindset for quite some time, or even the wrong job.

"The second question I ask myself is whether or not this person deserves the feedback," Kelly said. "This sounds harsh, but there are people who do not warrant the investment. This is a valuable piece of advice that takes effort on your part, so make that investment with care."

Why hold back just because they don't deserve it? The echoing distortion that the person in question has might travel through the force and could do more harm than good, but more important, this question is really about the giver.

"To question whether a recipient deserves feedback also gets your head in the right place," Kelly continued, "to make sure you see the value in the person you plan to offer feedback to."

The advice to consider whether the person deserves feedback is critical. Most of us can think of a few times that we regret when we could have helped someone by saying something but it would have cost us too much personally.

Several stories I heard followed the same course; anyone could insert his or her problem and coworkers' names and they would fit. One leader's story illustrates this well.

"I had a CEO friend I felt was making a mistake," the man remembered. "It wasn't immediately threatening to the company, but he deserved to avoid having to wait and figure it out on his own. At first, it seemed he knew what he was doing and had good reasons. I kept my mouth shut."

After a painful few years and an unpleasant life for the company's managers, the man saw in a meeting a glimpse of the CEO's uncertainty. He racked his brain again for ways to tell the executive without cornering himself. He wasn't interested in starting what might seem like a petty discussion about sour grapes and hurt the relationship. The person kept quiet because he didn't want to make the investment.

"All the safe, politically correct feedback continued to come openly from people who were seeing the same concern but were only talking candidly behind the scenes," the man remembered. "Productivity suffered. Everyone continued whitewashing and celebrating any great news around the topic, in spite of what was really going on. All of us wrote off his action as something he knew more about than we did."

This example, like so many similar stories, has a common ending: After significant damage to morale and projects, the CEO eventually uncovered his own blind spot—but the information came too late.

In such stories, the person needing feedback later asks why we withheld what we saw. The person does *not* say, "Oh, I'm sure glad you kept your mouth shut; the last thing I would've wanted you to do was help me earlier." If a person deserves feedback and will take it in the right spirit, give it to him early enough so he can use it. We shouldn't let regret be our only teacher.

For some leaders, more positive feedback is a way of padding their own egos, sharing the benefit of their experience or superior capabilities. Such ego-based feedback is the hardest to take, and the person receiving it likely doesn't deserve it. Check your ego and if necessary, keep the thought to yourself; no one deserves this kind of feedback, and the recipient likely won't listen anyway.

Third Question: Will They Receive It?

After deciding if the person deserves feedback, we need to discern the recipient's state of listening.

"The third question to answer for yourself," Kelly continued, "is whether they will receive the feedback. You may have something to offer, they may deserve it, but, for whatever reason, you know it won't be heard. Are they open enough? Are they humble enough to consider the feedback at least a little objectively? Are they skilled enough to understand a new technique? Sometimes, to understand feedback, you have to have something like an out-of-body experience and see things from a different point of view."

Most CEOs are complimentary of salespeople in general and say that they have worked with "some amazing salespeople whom I've really enjoyed." A CEO told me that he once heard that the chances of making a sale drop significantly when the sales guy talks more than 30 percent of the time. He told me of one of the most successful salespeople he's ever worked with, but the salesperson talked every chance he got. On calls, the CEO could see occasions when listening would have really made more sense for the rep.

"I flew out with this sales guy to meet with a large pharmacy retailer," he said, "and this guy talked up a storm. They didn't buy. After, I remember how the sales guy went off on how dumb they must be to not get what we offered. It seems like some salespeople—especially the good ones—take rejection personally. I thought the retailer was making a business decision, 'It stinks, but oh well.' The sales guy acted like they were calling him ugly—it was extremely personal."

The level of the salesperson's anger didn't seem healthy to the team, but it sometimes seems that all the good reps tend to take losses personally.

"I guess they can afford therapy," the CEO said. "Anyway, this salesperson was going off on how dumb the retailer was, and I said, 'Maybe we should have listened more about that one issue, it seemed like there was something there.' It wasn't the best timing on my part. I didn't edit myself and ask, 'Will the valuable feedback be received?'"

Some people will take feedback at certain times and not others. Unfortunately, this wasn't one of those times for the rep. You have to ask yourself if recipients are able to take it. They might deserve it, and you might have something valuable to offer, but they just won't receive it. It bounces off them as if they were Teflon. After a feedback experience or two with someone, you'll get a strong sense of when feedback will be received. How do you really tell if someone is open to feedback? I asked Alan, a friend of mine in a sales support function, when he might be visibly open to feedback from a salesperson.

"I would probably have body language which would be different. If I weren't open, I might show signs of stonewall. These might be visible symptoms of being emotionally injured, having a recent setback, feeling threatened—or I might just be in a mood that's lacking humility. My signs of acceptance might be visible expressions of trust, desire for continuing relationship, or outright curiosity. If a person is open, then consideration turns back to the giver of the feedback.

Fourth Question: Am I Too Focused on Being Nice?

What's the final consideration before letting words slip from your mouth? Check your sincerity, to consider if your focus is on being nice or if you are confident about being able to help. You have thought carefully and have decided that the intended feedback is valuable, the person deserves it, and it will be received; now, it's time to talk.

As Kelly put it, "Get clear, get confident, or at least comfortable with the investment you are about to make."

When Sales Blazers know that they can help, there is no hesitation or sugarcoating—no shying away. If you feel yourself hesitating, don't offer feedback. If you're feeling that the feedback will be painful, change your mindset before giving it.

When someone wades into a conversation with an extra-sweet preamble, they are digging a hole. The provider of feedback may be saying, "I've just got to tell you that you're an awesome guy, you're great," but the recipient is hearing, "This is going to really hurt," or worse, they don't see it coming and they think you really are offering a compliment—which you then take back. Insincere sugarcoating will waste your investment and probably do more harm than good.

Kelly offered a great metaphor for this.

"Think of a doctor giving you a shot," he said. "Does he flinch? No way. If the doctor just came out of the classroom, he or she may flinch, but who wants that doctor? My doctor flinched once—20 years later I still remember it.

"As a confident and caring leader, why would you hesitate or flinch when offering help?"

Sincere, relevant feedback that is positive brings healing perspective.

"When I am coaching a new manager," Kelly explained, "who may be apprehensive about giving feedback, I ask, 'What is your favorite ice cream?' People always answer that question in a completely clear, matter-of-fact way. That is the voice of feedback—matter-of-fact and clear."

When it's right for a leader to give feedback, duty calls. Feedback is about offering healing, not sympathy. If you flinch, if you're thinking, "It's going to hurt," it will. Once you're past the point of deciding you have something to offer to someone who deserves it and who will receive it, then feedback isn't criticism. It's honor and respect.

STEP 2: USE THE MENTAL-ERROR CONCEPT

If you have answered the questions and determined that feedback is warranted, the *mental-error concept* can help guide you toward either constructive or negative feedback. We will explore the mental-error concept as the key to three relevant categories of feedback situations. There are times when encouragement is needed and times when critique is needed. There are a few times when pointed criticism is warranted, and there are times to nip mistakes in the bud. Before discussing feedback on great performance, let's take a look at how to treat two different types of errors that salespeople make: mental errors and performance errors (see Figure 7.1).

Mental Errors Deserve Negative Feedback

A *mental error* is failing at the familiar. When a performer has succeeded with a familiar action in a familiar situation for years, it

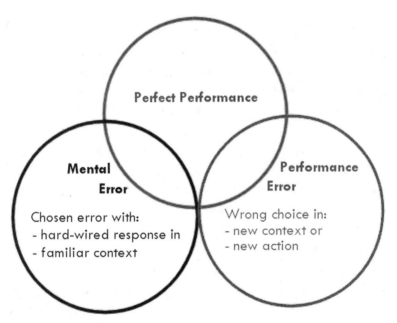

Figure 7.1 Feedback Zones

becomes second nature—like brushing your teeth correctly in your bathroom. Failing to perform circles and up and down brushes is not a sudden impulse; it is a choice to ignore years of experience. It is a mental error. It's like failing to pick up the phone for six months, after being in sales for 20 years. There is rarely time for this kind of negligence by a performer, and a leader's feedback may need to be negative in order to be effective.

A good leader gets on mental errors immediately to prevent the mistake from becoming permanent behavior or, worse, spreading through the team. The most valuable feedback on mental errors comes in response to specific actions, such as making no prospect calls for a month or saying something highly inappropriate on a call. For example, repeatedly missing realistic quotas for which a salesperson has the tools to deliver falls into the mental-error category.

Sales professionals know that low sales results year after year are counter to what their careers have always been about. Failure to deliver realistic goals year after year qualifies as something that requires negative feedback. One Sales Blazer described the seemingly obvious need for feedback on poor performance.

"Previous managers hadn't ever told two of my former reps that they needed to bring their sales results up in certain areas," she said. "Performance that was lower than quota year after year was left to speak for itself.

"Their previous manager should have offered feedback. When they were fired, the reps were shocked and threatened a lawsuit," she continued. "Some feedback may have triggered a behavior change or, at least, discouraged a lawsuit. Managers who are too nice, without really thinking what individuals need, do their people a disservice."

Missing quota once can happen and is not a mental error but more of a "performance error," and should be treated differently.

Performance Errors Deserve Constructive Feedback

Performance errors are mistakes made unintentionally by people when faced with an unfamiliar expectation or a new situation. Focusing on technique is difficult while struggling up a learning curve. Great leaders give carefully constructive feedback on new tasks or in new situations to accelerate learning and improve focus.

Great leaders recognize that moments and momentum are precious in a performance setting. When they see a performance error, they give motivational, specific instruction. It isn't helpful to explode the decibel level, positive or negative, in the workplace. Choosing between criticism and encouragement is a choice that Sales Blazers make thoughtfully. They understand what constructive feedback looks like. We will discuss celebrating perfect performance in the next section and chapter. But positive, detailed feedback about future action is key.

Perfect Performance

Sometimes the right feedback for a perfect performance can change a career and a life. One Sales Blazer told me of an experience in the early days of his career back in 1979. He had been wondering if selling was really the career for him. In a meeting with his manager and a banking client, the client offered a trip to Hawaii and other inappropriate benefits to the rep to replace commissions if he would get him out of an ATM contract at the branches.

The offer came at a moment in the young career when the rep was disenchanted with sales because a more senior salesperson in the office always seemed dishonest behind the scenes.

"I'm sorry," he bravely said. "I can't accept your generous offer."

He did so thinking he'd lose a lot of commission and not really knowing for sure if it was even against policy. The manager knew they would let the client out of the contract anyway, and pulled the rep aside as they left the building.

The rep expected a scolding, but instead the manager took a different approach.

"That was the most amazing thing I've ever seen," he said. "You've got a bright future. You keep that up."

The manager told him in detail how he could make honesty work. That feedback gave him a new hope in his chosen sales profession that he has never lost.

Kelly provided some important insights into offering constructive feedback of any type.

"You have to build up, not tear down," he said. "If you have that in your heart, then it works. If you can say, 'This guy's just awesome, he's excellent, and where he's headed generally is harmonious with where I see him,' you'll make a better impact. This works because the person you're talking to has a sense that you hold them in high regard, even though you're asking them to do things differently. They can tell your intentions are positive."

STEP 3: OFFER THE RSVP STYLE OF CONSTRUCTIVE FEEDBACK

We now understand the conditions for giving feedback and withholding it, and whether to be negative or constructive. We hear the term *constructive criticism* all the time, but the expression is really a contradiction in terms. If being constructive is warranted, build the future without using the past as a tool to tear everything down.

That said, there's more to feedback than flattery. Effective feedback acts as a prompt for specific action, guidance in a sales cycle, and can even act as its own reward for success or as punishment for failure. It reinforces or discourages what people do.

Thinking of feedback as an RSVP (please respond) invitation makes it easy to remember the key differences between a Sales Blazer's feedback and fruitless feedback. For example, an RSVP invitation feels exclusive and very specifically describes an exciting, future event. Also, the RSVP requires a second communication—a response—a two-way feedback loop. From the recipient's point of view, the RSVP feedback should feel personally inviting and exclusive, but it requires more attention. A specific commitment within a particular timeframe is what makes it powerful.

What does this really mean out in the sales field? One great rep didn't research a prospect very well and didn't leave enough time to practice the presentation and, consequently, blew it.

After the appointment, a Sales Blazer on his team focused on the next presentation and made specific, unassuming suggestions about how to prepare for that presentation, without focusing on the previous failure. The specific recommendations were followed by encouragement that included reasons the leader knew this rep could successfully execute the new steps.

Finally, the Sales Blazer requested that the rep follow up on a specific date to tell him about the great preparation, then again after the results of the next presentation. Obviously, in a managerial situation this can be more of a positive assignment than an enthusiastic request, but even a request holds magic. The rep remembered the request much better than usual comments. He felt more positive about the work because it was much more relevant and presented well; he looked forward to the follow-up to brag a little.

RSVP Characteristics

- Invitation to take new steps, not criticizing the past
- Exclusive feeling of excitement, benefit—something offered to a select few
- A focus on detailed performance on a specific date
- A response requested for commitment and follow-up

Selling the Comeback

Feedback should come in the form of an invitation. One of the most important ideas about the concept of offering feedback came from Raja, a Sales Blazer in financial services with whom I spoke.

"I try to give encouragement with meat," she said. "When I was a rep, Tate, one of the greatest managers I ever had, would do something really important whenever he could tell you were down or just not doing your best."

Raja explained that she tries to do the same for people on her team. Instead of kicking salespeople when they're down, she sells them on their eventual success and then commits them to it.

Raja continued, "Once Tate called me and said, 'You may not remember it, but last year you were behind, too. You were

$100,000 down the last few weeks. You probably didn't feel as bad as you do now because, at the time, everyone around you was saying you were a proposal machine. You were on a kick to progress everything. You know when you are on a roll and doing all the right things, falling behind a little isn't the end of the world. Sure you're down $150,000 this year, but last year, with similar timing, you didn't just make up the $100,000, you had a big account come in during the last week, ultimately worth $145,000. You can absolutely do this again. We can do this again. You know we can, and we both know what it will take. I'll make you a deal. If you will get enough real proposals presented, I'll chase my independent buddy around three times over the next few weeks and try to get two opportunities out of him. Do we have a deal to call each other in three weeks to check in?'"

Not only did Tate express his belief in Raja, he put his trust on the line by making a deal with her. By the way, Tate did bring Raja a new sale and she did the rest, making her goal that year. RSVP feedback includes follow-up that works.

Examples: Making It Look Easy in the Field

I almost put together a slick, decision-tree diagram to describe all this. But that kind of complicated, written process wasn't really what I observed of Sales Blazers—it was instantaneous. It was developed intuition more than a process. If you could slow it down, the three steps again would confirm this: Offering feedback is worth it (or not), is constructive (or not), and includes two-way commitments.

Sales Blazers instinctively understand that a moment of feedback can go a long way. For example, Kim watched from the sidelines as his parent company, GM, brought in a consultant to run the dealership. They quickly went from the top 100 in the nation to the bottom 10. Finally, Kim took control with a new approach. The dealership bounced back to a spot in the top 50 dealerships for the brand. I talked to Kim and his team.

"The consultant was bright but tried to cookie-cutter a situation and a group of people who are all different," Kim said.

Kim explained that in his work leaders have to have a hands-on approach. Because the consultant hadn't been hands-on in his market, they had far less measurement that really mattered.

Kim explained that in his work you need proper measurement and feedback, and with it creativity and sincerity—sincerity is a must.

"It really comes down to giving constant feedback on relevant standards," Kim said. "We're on the same properties, so you can't smother people, but because new things are coming out all the time, you have to be able to coach your people and give them feedback. Walk in their shoes before you pick them apart. I never degrade or embarrass someone publicly for making an honest mistake. I always try to see things from their perspective first. If you don't, you may never get their focus back.

"The cardinal 'sandwich' rule is that if you need to give feedback you find something positive, then you can give the negative, then positive feedback again to build them back up, like a sandwich. But it has to be genuine. Show them they can do it because they've done it before; basically you prove to them that they can do this and you'll keep them ready to sell. Then, I check back. Now they expect feedback."

Sales Blazers told me of former managers who were incredibly structured with their feedback. They, too, agreed with the sandwich approach, but stressed that it can't be too structured, fake, or mechanical.

"My former manager would give a compliment that everyone knew was transparent—made up," recalled one leader. "Soon, it became clear that when he said anything nice about someone, there was some crappy feedback coming. Everyone knew—even his peers—that when he said something positive about you, you better duck, because here comes some scathing criticism. It became so mechanical that everyone stopped listening."

> *Reticence insulates and hides poor performance:* Sales Blazers clear huge amounts of insulating silence that may have built up for years around causes of poor performance in teams. The unspoken gets spoken in the right way with RSVP feedback.

Kelly offered a double dose of feedback. "Interestingly, I had an issue with giving feedback about feedback to two of my managers," he remembered. "People from one team were afraid of the manager of the other team. I asked the manager of the first team, 'Have you told him that?' He said, 'No!' I said, 'Well, let's go tell him.' 'Uh, well . . . ,' the manager hesitated. But we stopped at the other manager's office and the first manager, trying to offer feedback, started saying, 'You know you're so great, you do such a great job,' dancing around the issue. The second manager was thinking, 'What's this guy saying?' Very few people have such poor instincts that they don't know when someone is sugarcoating."

225

Kelly continued, "I interrupted, 'You know what?' I said, 'Sometimes when these guys have something to tell you, they're scared of your title.' I just said exactly what was there. The manager was disarmed by the honest intent, and we were able to have a real conversation without all the sugarcoating and misinformation.

"By stating the truth, we could move on and create value and benefit, as opposed to filling the moment with what's disingenuous. Then, I asked the first manager to report back in a month specifically on how things had become better."

THE RSVP DIFFERENCE

Mediocre managers criticize poor performance. Sales Blazers consider whether a situation or an action is new before criticizing. They specify the needed change and invite the rep to report back on the personal benefits gained from success. They also invite the salesperson to follow up on progress by a logical date, because great feedback feels like an RSVP invitation. Most important, they don't wait until an annual or quarterly review to do all this; they do it now.

Another lesson I've learned from Sales Blazers is that if you invite feedback, you get it. I have a personal example of RSVP feedback that one of my coworker heroes, named Rulon, gave to me.

At one point in my career, I was sitting in my office and Rulon, a vice president of sales, popped in to talk about a possible opportunity to sell some services to a sales organization. At the end of our discussion, he said, "Hey do you have a second that I can share a thought with you?"

"Sure," I said.

"I think you do great things here. And you know, if you made yourself more visible with the executives of this company, I think you could have a shot at a higher executive position. But you need to suggest it yourself and then make yourself more visible inside the company."

I was flattered and then I bored him with my valiant intent to add real value in the field, market, and economy instead of wasting time self-promoting in the halls of my own company.

"Wait a minute," Rulon replied. "I understand that, but you should consider adding value to everyone, including people you work with—I'm just talking about the right amount. I'm just saying I think you've got a shot if you want it and you should figure out how to take it and make your intent and efforts felt inside as well as outside the company. Think about it and if you want to talk about it I'll be in next week."

Of course I went home to my wife bragging about the nice things Rulon had said, because I hadn't even been thinking along these lines. Finally, a while later, it dawned on me that he had really been suggesting that, regardless of what I want, I need to change my ways internally—that's just not how it came across. It wasn't all upside; there was some potential downside without a change, but he'd made it an invitation for something positive.

I spent a few days thinking about working better to "add value to everyone." I spent some time over the next few weeks enrolling people, even the previously less interested, in a vision I saw for my project. I asked for their feedback, invited them to help if they wanted, and even invited some criticism. I experienced the most enjoyable two weeks of my year, if nothing else.

This experience all happened because Rulon didn't hesitate to give feedback that could really help. He realized I was in a new situation and offered feedback in the form of an opportunity with genuine encouragement. Finally, he told me when he wanted to talk about it again, which opened up a two-way communication to ensure progress—all from someone to whom I didn't even report. He quickly gave me a shot of positive value and didn't hesitate or give it to someone else for fear of hurting me.

RSVP Feedback's Place

At this point, we have given and received feedback, guiding the team to success through all the previous strategies. In the next chapter, we will learn to better reward and perpetuate the growth we achieve.

Strategy Summary—RSVP Feedback

1. Decide if giving feedback is even right in the situation.
2. Determine if the person's mistake was a choice involving a situation *and* an action that are second-nature—a mental error. If not, don't criticize; instead, invite.
3. Advise how to close the gap between performance and expectations.
4. Motivate confidence in success using the person's history of similar successes.
5. Invite the person to succeed during the next similar opportunity and benefit personally.
6. Request an RSVP: Set a date and request a response about progress to create a two-way feedback loop.

Heighten Reward Potency

THE STRATEGY

Heighten the effect on revenue with a potent appreciation and rewards program that celebrates achievement with self-actualizing awards—*Heighten Reward Potency.*

> *What we will accomplish in this chapter:* We will describe a better purpose for providing incentives for others to act. We will explain how better expertise and celebration can enhance results. We will learn about appreciation and rewards that contribute to the personal success of clients and salespeople and that spur results. We will see how this last strategy fits with the others.

PROBLEMS: POOR PURPOSE, EXECUTION, AND REWARDS

Rewards are a daily part of any sales rep's job. We try to show appreciation to clients, to members of the team, and, for managers, the staff. Regardless of your budget, you can use rewards to motivate people to respond in a positive, revenue-enhancing way.

Rewards outside of normal compensation usually lose impact if they don't have a clear purpose, a smooth execution, or a motivating goal. Rewards won't have much effect if the people you work with feel you are simply doing something you've always done. Appreciation can actually distract from results if it is executed and delivered incorrectly. Worst of all, it may

232

become irrelevant to successful salespeople or customers if they begin to say, "I don't need another one of those. I already have half a dozen. Don't they think if I wanted another one I'd just go buy it?"

SOLUTION: BETTER PURPOSE, EXECUTION, AND REWARDS

Sales Blazers give a new, higher potency to rewards programs to increase revenue. The differences they provide include:

1. *Better purpose*—appreciation of individual successes while celebrating revenue successes
2. *Better execution*—using professionals in five required disciplines to improve performance
3. *Better rewards*—offering rewards that contribute to individual pursuit, not just reward it

A BETTER PURPOSE

Adding personal purpose to your rewards program is powerful. Earlier, we explored how to spark a performance pursuit by intermingling a person's work with deeply held ambitions. To heighten reward potency means rewarding in ways that aid those same pursuits going forward. Passions last longer than whims, fads, and often brands; tapping into these passions is essential.

What does it take to understand just enough about people's pursuits that you've discovered in previous chapters to do this? Let's use sailing to illustrate.

Before I met a Sales Blazer named Robert, I knew nothing about sailing. Robert is a sales and marketing vice president for

HAAC, an architectural metal products firm with a *Who's Who* list of international clients. When his casting industry started moving all manufacturing overseas, he battened the hatches and sailed HAAC's revenue out of recession by taking an intense interest in what his people and clients really cared about.

What were Robert's passions beyond work, family, and spirituality? I told him I wasn't looking for a mere hobby, but for something into which he poured his heart, mind, time, and money.

"That's easy," he said. "I'm one of those fanatical sailors. We're not 'wannabe' sailors. Real sailors own serious boats, we race, or we stay up with what is happening in the sailing world. We make a pilgrimage every year to sail or restore boats in Maine.

> *Champion, but don't be an expert:* It's not important to become an expert at every pursuit that each of your colleagues follows. The important thing is to learn from the people you influence about the pursuit's highest achievements and desired tangibles, and then champion the cause. Learning about the highest echelons of a pursuit will let you avoid awkwardly telling a former opera singer about your own second year of voice lessons.

"When we get together with friends, the conversation ends up at which boats are being built, what classics are being restored, or what's the latest racing edge. Or one of us will rant about some truth we've discovered from a sea novel found in an obscure bookstore, or the latest article in a boat magazine."

Robert suggested that I would understand even better if I talked to Wid, a gentleman who had worked with him in the community.

Adding Lure to the Program

Can a pursuit affect daily motivation? Wid described the lure of his personal pursuit with a story.

"Sailing's in my blood. We were sailing the 80-mile race that used to go around Fremont Island. I was thinking, 'I absolutely love this unbelievable feeling.'"

The crew was flying along around midnight with their 32-footer heeled way over, marching it with the spinnaker up (the large triangular sail on the boom spar that swings away from the mainsail).

"It was pitch dark," Wid said. "We passed Fremont Island and were heading for a gap island with incredible wind. The wind was howling when we flew into it. It knocked us almost perpendicular to the water, with the boat standing straight up. It was crazy! We couldn't control the sheet [a line on the spinnaker], so we had to let it go right in the middle of the race."

The spinnaker whipped and flew like a flag from the front and out the back of the boat. The crew finally had to cut it loose because it was flapping in the wind; it took them a long time to get it under control and onto the boat.

"We were all yelling, ripping in the middle of the race," Wid continued. "We knew that if we broached [veered suddenly broadside], our mast could break right off." If the mast went into the water, the whole boat could whip around in a violent U-turn. "We hung on, and we finally made it." Wid smiled. "What a rush! Can you see why I'd do anything to sail?"

How do you add the strength of this kind of passion and individual recognition to rewards? Bring *internalization* into celebration after bringing it into work. Sales Blazers do more than promise commissions and merchandise for results; they reward passion with passion. They use the unique language of a person's personal pursuit in the celebration. For instance, a sailor's colleague would find a way to involve that rep's professional success *and* sailing success in the celebration. Let's take a look at how.

Figure 8.1 is a basic blueprint for a typical sales incentive program and will guide us through the explanation. The line beneath the pyramid shows a genuine relationship required for recognition. The layers indicate criteria for a career club; annual incentives; quarterly rewards; quick start, intermittent promotions, strong finish; and ad hoc incentives.

Career Club

Let's use our sailing example and a particular salesperson's unique passion for selling CRM (customer relationship management) software to explore what this career club language

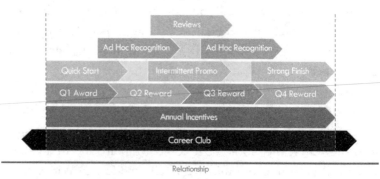

Figure 8.1 Performance Incentives Blueprint

might look like. Career clubs build on a long-term relationship with successful performers, and deeply bond them with the company. But is it really possible to have a deep relationship with Robert or Wid without acknowledging sailing?

Career clubs celebrate several years of exemplary professional achievement against company qualifiers, such as three years of quota achievement. However, this message reaches only part of the person's goals. It says, "You've earned your way into *our* club, so *we're* admitting you."

The plaques, checks, and trips with associates are really about building work relationships and offering esteem. What if we heightened the club affiliation to include the individual's life-long and personal career aspirations? What if we sold database management software, not CRM, but we acknowledged that the company buys into the salesperson's unique brand of success—CRM expertise *and* sailing?

Suppose that individual self-concept and self-actualization are included in the language and purpose of the club. Then the *salesperson* would own the entire achievement, including the company criteria in the background. In this example, recognizing the unique individual is what connects CRM and sailing with the company achievement.

For those who have achieved professional status in unique ways, the career club becomes a place where society, as well as a company, can bestow recognition. The club recognizes the salesperson's CRM expertise, but—for a sailor, for example, it also recognizes sailing's contribution and professional qualifications. It celebrates the salesperson surpassing company criteria in both industry and sailing terms.

We will talk more about rewards later, but the rewards could be sailing courses, equipment, or a rare excursion that might even stretch the person's ability. Once someone you are working with is inspired to continued pursuit, she will remember that you were the one who helped her get there. In addition, you will be helping to align the company's goals with the individual's personal life.

A first-class career club recognizes individuals' pursuits both inside and outside the company. A presentation at the sample company that sells database management software might include something like "Yes, Taft ranked in the top 10 for a fifth year to enter Career Club. But to put this in perspective, Taft's unique efforts would also rank him in the top 10 percent of all professional CRM salespeople anywhere. We are honored to have him creating a vision for our database clients with CRM installations. I've seen how he's used his salty sailing skills of focus, strategy, and teamwork to gain and serve clients well. He takes the teamwork of a crew very seriously. He's even helped us on accounts in Maine, which is outside his territory."

People who interact with Sales Blazers praised this new direction of recognition as championing their individual causes. Ask yourself: "Would I rather be congratulated for a significant achievement in terms defined by my profession, *and* by a worthy friend, or only for goals understood by a single corporate entity and a distant manager?"

> *One dictionary definition of recognition:* Coming to understand something clearly and distinctly.

A clear desire of career salespeople is to be genuinely appreciated as individual professionals rather than just to be offered trinkets and typical travel as part of a group.

Annual Success

Chris, a former vice president at Computer Associates and now CEO of Vintela, Inc., created what he calls an annual "Wonder Trip" and other rewards to lead Vintela, a start-up, to a multi-million dollar sale of the company.

"Most receive a bonus, major merchandise, or all three," Chris said. "But I knew one of my salespeople loved cycling, so when we went to lunch to celebrate his success, guess what we talked about? I also got him on a ride with some professional athletes. It meant a lot to him."

When it comes to annual incentives, why not incorporate the individual's performance pursuit, as in our example of sailing and CRM expertise? Celebrate and facilitate self-actualizing achievements instead of merely saying, "You earned the incentive trip," or "You made quota."

As salespeople we are focused, as we should be, on succeeding with sales, but what about those consultative teams who have helped us get there? Would volunteering to contribute this kind of communication at the end of the period in the department next door do any good? Absolutely. Nothing will accelerate the performance you receive from others next period like some gratitude shown formally.

How would this language play for a client? Consider a thank you note addressed to your contact's CEO or direct supervisor when the contact achieves significant results for you. We celebrate success in terms of individuals we claim to lead wherever they may be, and we can weave in their self-actualization goals. The company or department criteria remain; they just sit more in the background. Let's look, for example, at short-term success.

Short-Term Successes

Quarterly contests and incentives for a strong start or a strong finish are usually in addition to other short-term rewards such as active expectations. Short-term recognition feeds esteem and belonging and can be a little harder to mingle with long-term passions. The message is usually more private but can still involve short-term, career-building goals:

"We value your quickness in picking new things up to accomplish (A) for yourself and your customers, and benefit the company a great deal, too. We count on you because you continue to become a stronger and stronger (B)."

Personal achievements deserve more frequent praise, given in a less public manager–salesperson conversation.

Informal recognition and intermittent contests near the top of the performance recognition program are usually for short occasional promotions, product launches, specific activities, and so on.

Mary's people, at one of the largest IT outsourcing firms in the world, say that Mary proved a model leader when the training center's sales increased 19 times over previous revenue. They attribute her strong leadership to celebrating the individual. "No matter how small the contribution toward success, it is acknowledged and appreciated. Encouragement to accomplish goals is always available, because she pays attention to the details." Congratulations for these smaller steps include rewarding active expectations; they may involve all types of goals.

Why go to such lengths to position the purpose, language, and rewards? To continue the performance pursuit and to bond the team, the leader, and his or her championing company. We have gone to great lengths to change the direction of revenue;

we must continue to work on the momentum. To the leader it may not seem like a big deal to be a little more individualized, but from the other person's perspective, it feels huge.

Rewards and recognition are related, but they are two entirely different things. Just as awards and rewards accelerate performance, adding appreciation by recognizing unique individuals adds more fuel to the fire. Perhaps Adrian Gostick and Chester Elton said it best in their book *The Carrot Principle*: "It may sound like magic, but it isn't. The relationship between a management accelerant and improved business results is highly predictable. In fact, an accelerant is the missing ingredient that will bridge the gap between where your team is now and where it can be. And in the workplace, there is no accelerator with more impact than purpose-based recognition."

Gostick and Elton's numbers prove the accelerating effect. They worked with the Jackson Organization to conduct one of the most extensive and in-depth studies ever performed on workplace productivity. The study quantified connections among employee satisfaction, business outcomes, and recognition. Appreciating individuals' uniqueness and appreciating their contributions both help appreciate revenue.

Better Purpose, Better Connection

Adding new, overarching purpose to celebrations creates a strong loyalty among the leader, team members, and the company. Thoughts I heard expressed by the teammates who had been shown appreciation by Sales Blazers included, "I'd go to the well for him," and "I work my heart out for her." Such sentiments don't develop from the basic preaching of sales goals.

We should not rely solely on our people's desire to please the company or us. Rewarding passion with passion is critical to heighten reward potency and boost revenue.

One salesperson I observed loved to sing. She performed in clubs, concerts, and choirs. Her comments illuminate the impact of understanding a rep's passions.

"One year I was in a music competition with one of the groups I perform with," she said. "Every night it felt like we were holding on for dear life as the next cut was announced. Every time we performed, it felt like we were in the middle of natural harmony. I swear we floated, in pitch dark, as the lights went on each night. Feeling our team blending together, seeing the faces of the audience light up—it's an incredible experience.

"Working with people who understand each other like no one else is a rush. On a stage, you bond quicker than you do at almost any other time. That's what a competition will do. Singing is connected to our real beauty as people. The room is quiet except for our small ensemble, so you can actually hear each person, and you get to know them through their voices. In fact, you have to, for many reasons."

The salesperson explained how singing helps her connect with others as a professional also.

"Singing connects humans," she said. "People who sing at a professional level experience something unique. When you are invited to be in someone's group, it's rare. Through the years, you talk about good times, funny times . . . performing those disastrous arrangements, some of the trips, and gutsy competitions. It is an honor, a bonding, a brotherhood, a sisterhood.

"As we talk, different interests and experiences within singing add texture and build the bond between different skill sets because we all share something. Connecting with singing is connecting with me."

Could someone wanting to motivate this person succeed by always bringing up overdue next steps, quota, money, their own sales, or how great the firm's mission statement is, and then offering a celebration that conflicts with a major concert? Or would someone do better by also tracking, congratulating, and even contributing to this well-rounded accomplishment? The answer I heard loud and clear was that Sales Blazers who champion personal purpose with related rewards motivate professional success. They also get help.

BETTER EXECUTION—A REFLECTION OF PROFESSIONAL EXPERTISE

The second way to heighten reward potency is to use the right expertise. Let's return to sailing for just a moment and note the unexpected parallel between Robert and Wid's sailing passion and gaining requisite expertise.

"It takes an expert skipper, crew, and the right equipment to win a sailing race," Wid said. "The whole crew needs to know the rules of winning: how to maneuver, how to avoid lulls in the wind, how to get the vessel to respond. You need to be able to read the weather. *Most of all, you have to know yourself and what you can handle.* These boats can handle 2,000 pounds, but if you make the wrong move, the wind just bends and wrecks it like it was nothing."

Perhaps the best example of someone putting the right crew and the right program together is Dennis Conner, the great skipper of our era, who led his team through an unprecedented eight America's Cup campaigns, won more than 100 America's

Cup Trial races, and won the America's Cup itself in 1974, 1980, 1987, and 1988. How did he do it? With the right crew, the right equipment, and the right plan.

> *Dennis Conner on the right crew and the right technology:* "With these new boats and our veteran crew of American sailors, I feel this is one of the best campaigns I've ever put together . . . which is true testament to how hard our whole team has worked to make this day possible."

The Pitch on Expertise

You deserve the right crew and the right technology for your performance program. Now that we understand how powerful the right purpose can be, it's important to understand that a motivational environment created by an effective leader includes a well-run reward program. I spoke to two other incentive experts about what we should keep in mind in planning an effective incentive program. One was Michelle Smith, who has led several associations in the incentive industry. She pointed out, "Well-designed programs have a substantially higher impact on revenue than poorly planned programs with all the same trappings."

I observed in-house programs that were managed with spreadsheets rather than with enterprise-class software. Some were launched with incomplete e-mails or color flyers that were disbursed haphazardly, and, as a result, made a poor first impression. On an ongoing basis, they had no impact. These programs often had unrealistic goals, and the rewards did not inspire the sales force.

Ed Robbins, who has also led several incentive associations and companies, related to me that many firms have resources to execute reward programs, but they sometimes delegate the tasks to a single administrator.

"Truly motivational programs use distinct professional capabilities," Ed pointed out. The five distinct professional capabilities are these:

1. Sales leadership partnered with program planners
2. Professional marketing, including training
3. Experienced program management
4. Comprehensive sales performance technology
5. Awards sourced to contribute to self-actualization

One story told by a sales event organizer I spoke to illustrates the impact that expertise can have. He told of inviting an experienced crew to help him launch a program. Instead of receiving a color flyer or e-mail, the salespeople were loaded onto buses early one morning, ending up and exiting the buses some distance away on a small plateau in the desert.

Puzzled, they watched the buses drive away as giant, mechanical-looking creatures (acrobats on stilts and wearing costumes) crawled over the horizon and converged on the sales force. The creatures came close enough to be recognized as symbols of program criteria that had been carefully planned by program designers (specialized business analysts) who had access to experts in all five disciplines of performance improvement.

The event continued with a highly entertaining and motivating presentation of expectations and measures, and ended with a parade of rewards—a far cry from colored e-mails with hokey themes. Don't despair if your program isn't running smoothly; it's not too late. Also, don't worry if you have only a small discretionary budget and little time; your role and expertise are still critical.

Small works, too: This principle of applying the five areas of expertise work on even the smallest scale with the least expensive awards—you just may have to consider the five areas as standards of your own professionalism rather than of actual professionals. You may not get experts chomping at the bit, but learning about pursuits costs nothing, and an appropriately small reward may not cost much more. I gave a poster signed by Dennis Conner that I got at a trade show to a dear friend, "Captain" Morris. At the time, I didn't even know who Dennis Conner was. The poster now hangs on my friend's boat, and he mentions his appreciation every year when he takes me sailing with his crew.

One Sales Blazer with little budget for recognition said, "Some corporations' structure or size does limit frontline managers' ability to personalize incentives creatively. Sometimes we don't get large discretionary funds for an incentive model. The fear is that we are going to waste money at the frontline and we're not going to get the return on the investment. What some of my peers and I do is try to figure out what is most important to each individual. I really make it a priority to look at all the options to show appreciation that I can add. I put the pieces together to maximize those things I have available. I reward what is most important to each individual. How these incentives express themselves is unique to each person, but it varies from public recognition to private appreciation, to financial compensation, to family weekends at a ski resort—everything is different, depending on the individual."

An Example of Experts in the Field

A properly designed and executed reward program doesn't just benefit the client or rep, it also creates huge financial gains. Christine, a sales vice president, has produced revenue growth in multiple industries. She was hired at a performance company because of her success in expanding and diversifying her previous firm's sales. The proportion of automotive sales to total sales dropped from 100 percent to a safer, diversified 25 percent, and she added over $10 million to total revenue in the process—two key objectives. Christine offers insights on what one often hears from experts serving the best sales organizations.

"I'll give you an example of professional impact. We had a client who was a manufacturer of recreational vehicles ranging in price up to $500,000 per unit. They'd had the same incentive program for years. The goals were outdated and the rewards lame. Salespeople forgot the program even existed. Something had to change. The client's product sold exclusively through dealers, and they needed to get the other salespeople selling our client's products instead of competing brands and show our appreciation."

Her business analysts' initial assessment and planning helped her team find out who the salespeople really were, what excited them and what didn't, and what tools they needed to win. To drive sales, the team couldn't just rely on the same earnings program with a standard selection of name-brand awards—the usual ironing boards and blenders. They needed to put together a custom selection of awards that would really appeal to the salespeople.

The partnership between experts and leaders comes into play in taking the awards beyond demographics and down to the individual level. If managers can understand the profile of each individual, and provide awards or at least mention awards in the program that will really help him or her get to the next level personally as well as professionally, the leader will get the individual's attention.

"The custom reward selection for our client ranged from $100 to lucrative $10,000 awards," Christine explained. "If they achieved, they could also join additional contests to achieve accelerators and possibly triple their rewards. The sales force really went after it and had a blast moving that product. We got the rewards so dialed in that we could almost gauge exactly for the client how many more units would sell by upping the 'spiff' during a particular month, and at what point returns would diminish."

To promote the program, Christine put her marketing experts to work. There hadn't been much effort to market the program effectively to salespeople. They knew they needed the hearts of the frontline leaders and sales champions in order to get everyone focused and excited. They did big splashes, at which every manager at every location received something called a "launch in a box."

"Inside the 'launch in a box' were posters, location prizes, brochures, ads for registration, and other exciting tangibles," Christine reported. "These reinforced the program that would go to these key players, and a description of the personal opportunities it presented. The first thing they saw was a brochure spelling out their manager's commission for team participation in addition to increasing sales. We kept it going, and coordinated it with the client's normal training and advertising—for example, we sent promotional bricks in conjunction with their Indy Car ads."

The team gave the managers tools that were simple and obvious to teach the salespeople about the benefits of selling the products. The recipients knew exactly how many rewards they could earn, and how they could maximize their other rewards by selling a mix of the client's products.

"We created training pieces for the salespeople," Christine continued, "to make sure they knew how to position our product favorably compared to the competition—to the point that they had actual selling language to use with customers. Normally, incentive firms don't go this far, and there's no way the client would have pulled all this off." Even if your company or your influence on programs is small, it's a good idea to get relevant professional advice before doling out awards.

Better Rewards—Actualization Awards

Now that you have brought an individual's purpose and new professionalism to the program, how do you continue a performance pursuit that we sparked early in the process? *Actualization awards*—rewards related to the pursuits being celebrated. This creates an emotional attachment for the person getting the reward. Internalization not only improves selling, it also improves the impact of the rewards.

Pay alone doesn't build the kind of bond we're looking for. Some programs focus on brand-name products instead of the rep. Total focus on corporate brands, selection, or cash helps mediocre managers avoid learning about their people. As we have discussed, work patterns have changed—it's time to engage companies in the individual, not just the other way around (see Figure 8.2).

Gain dedication by heightening the potency of rewards or the desirability of tokens of appreciation. Do it by focusing on the individual's own brand—self-actualization. What if you don't control the incentive or business gift resources? Let's see if an example can help.

I had an important colleague whom I wanted to thank in some small way for his impact on my work as I moved on. It couldn't be money or name brands—he had plenty of both.

A colleague named Randy suggested, "If you're trying to create a professional bond with him, I'll give you an idea. Find out what preoccupies him and give him one of two things. First, if you can find a vendor that can make a rarity that not even an enthusiast has, and it's within your price range, that's it. Second, if the rare find is more expensive than warranted, find the most

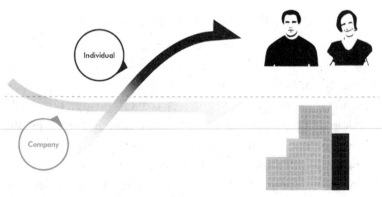

Figure 8.2 The New Engagement: A Rewards Redirect

rare, high-end journal on the topic and get him a subscription. Let's be clear, we are not talking about a $19.99 subscription, we're talking about the tabloid-sized $150 subscription—every pursuit has one of these big babies printed with a metallic, five-color process that covers the highest echelon of the topic."

I took Randy's advice. I already knew the man loved guns because of the debates his interest had created. I'd also seen computers with large holes shot in them around the office, and I'd heard the stories. Even though I'm not particularly a gun enthusiast, I found a vendor with a gift subscription to the best high-end gun magazine I could find that was tabloid size. I included a personal card, acknowledging what he'd done and how I admired what he also managed to achieve in his pursuit, and I wrapped the subscription ad up with a card.

"Who do you think he thinks about when that big beautiful book shows up every month?" Randy asked me, "There's the start to your bond."

I wanted to confirm that my experience with Randy wasn't getting me to hear things from Sales Blazers that they weren't really saying. I reviewed the data and asked Christine. Christine was the perfect person to ask because of her dual experience leading both salespeople and incentive programs.

I said to her, "Incentive administrators seem to care only about brand-name merchandise. But a brand represents the collective time, emotion, and money invested for a purpose—the total meaning of a company. Individuals have brands, too. It's their collective time, emotion, and money invested toward a unique purpose. I'm hearing that people care more about their own brand than name brands."

She confirmed that I was hearing the Sales Blazers correctly. "You're right, they care more about what has gone into creating their own personal identity than they care about any company's identity." Getting people energized about name brands is a safety net to keeping them passionate about extending their own brand—who they are.

"I've experienced a lot, which has created who I am," Christine said. "What I've wanted out of my career has changed, but I have passions that haven't changed. I am very passionate about our summer home. Nothing from Memorial Day weekend to Labor Day weekend will keep us from our summer home except a death or a marriage, and these better be in our family.

"My summer home story as a child is rich; it was the best childhood. We had so many kids and visitors. We spent the whole summer skiing, fishing, and talking around bonfires together. To me it was the best time of my life. I want to give that to my kids.

"My husband had heard me talk about my love for our summer home and, because he never had one, he wanted us to have one and to have that in our children's lives. We made huge sacrifices and bought a place in western Michigan. It's not a small island like my parents' summer home, but the love and impact continues. We don't have a phone . . . no TV, no Internet, and no cell phone coverage . . . it's just us. We do all the things I did as a kid. I'm very passionate about continuing this and making it matter. People that help build this somehow or even just understand it, I bond with. Can you imagine the difference in impact a leader has by offering *anything* adding to my summer home versus another TV incentive?" Consider the power of this type of tangible reward related to a pursuit.

A mistake that many sales experts make in trying to apply science to sales incentives happens when they try to train thinking humans the same way B. F. Skinner trained lab animals—with a generic "positive" reward, as we discussed in Chapter 5. Humans strive for more complex goals than chickens do. We need something besides this quarter's commissions, commodities, or pressure to get the full attention of those we seek to influence.

A friend of mine was a business owner and quite wealthy. Like successful salespeople, he had everything. I wanted to thank him for supporting my company during a successful year. This time I found a limited-edition, caste-bronze replica of the push plates from the front door at the old Chicago Stock Exchange building that no longer exists. In the old days, every morning, when traders stampeded onto the floor in Chicago, they pushed these plates to get in. It was the starting bell for the day. These push plates were incredibly hard to find, but when I did, they cost me less than $200. My friend didn't need another $200 or a trip to the mall with a gift certificate. This man loved to trade—this was an item that had personal meaning for him.

The most important thing to the majority of people is their own personal and professional brand—self-actualization. Imagine embedding messages and images of personal pursuit in trophies or paintings. Imagine commemorating on a ring, or an item of gold or crystal, an event of highly personal relevance.

Imagine rewarding a person's brand with self-actualizing equipment and unique travel with the proper, bonded crew. These are called *actualization awards* because they celebrate *and* facilitate real goal achievement. Redirecting conversations with people away from the company and toward their personal passions creates valuable new loyalty to the manager and to the company. And the manager becomes far more engaged, too.

Performance Barometer

Can leaders really individualize each reward offered, or do they have to settle by offering broad selections so people can do the individualizing themselves? There are three parts to the answer.

First, leaders don't have to settle; people often ask for a broad selection of awards because they want what they want, and typical businesspeople have no idea what's in the hearts of those they are trying to influence. It may be the thought that counts, but having this thought isn't common. We have now thoroughly described how Sales Blazers redirect their attention to their people's greatest desires, so it's important to use that new awareness to make rewards matter.

Second, vendors make money through the efficiencies of rewarding everyone using the same process, so they offer

Sales Blazer reward potency: In Chapter 6 we considered the work of Herbert Kelman in describing the process of *internalization*—the art of boosting performance by designing work to achieve self-actualization. In his work, Kelman described building the potency of a suggested activity to increase performance. He observed that selling the profound personal benefits of taking a particular course of action affected performance far more than mandates. Sales Blazers instinctively understand that designing appreciation and rewards targeted at passionate pursuits boosts results.

brand-name awards that should sound good to anyone. However, there are unique expressions of each pursuit, which can be bridged by leader communication or through a vendor. This is the reason for the manager–expert partnership to reach the individual level. Salespeople are motivated by the finesse of leaders in providing equipment and opportunity that support pursuits with a personal touch.

Third, there is a place for brand-name merchandise as a companion incentive or safety net, but only after you demonstrate to your salespeople your interest and your effort in helping them succeed as individuals. The least we can do for those we are trying to influence is find awards in the current program that we think fit their passions and mention those things to them.

THE DIFFERENCE: CHAMPION PERSONAL SUCCESS

Rob, the sailing VP of sales and marketing, made the point best when he asked me, "What would be more motivating to a salesperson who sails—the promise of another gift certificate; a rare, hand-blown glass barometer licensed from the collection at Mystic Seaport; or a unique lantern with a bronze hanger from the presidential yacht *Sequoia* or one of the old J-boats? Do you think we would work harder to have the barometer or lantern on our boat or in our study at home than another gift certificate? You better believe it."

The barometer may or may not be expensive, but leader–salesperson connection and perceived value are priceless. Rob continued, "I love working here. The people and experiences I have are literally more valuable than any paycheck I've received."

Sales Results

The sales results we have seen in the examples throughout this book speak for themselves. With the Sales Blazers Method we have reduced frustrations and explored aspirations. We have organized people and objectives and done some math on results. We have coached and given feedback for success. Now it's time to appreciate clients for effective action or reward a job well done with something that will make the success happen again. Actualization awards work to bond with clients, too.

Strategy Summary—Heighten Reward Potency

By *potency*, we mean maximizing the passionate desire to gain positive appreciation. The message received from salespeople is that the small additional bonus, the watch they could already buy if they wanted it, or the predictable group travel with the executives aren't personal enough by themselves. Now more than ever people want to be appreciated for their personal and career pursuits, not for just the corporate entity's tasks. To take your appreciation and reward program to the next level:

1. Heighten the potency of purpose by weaving personal pursuit with sales results.
2. Heighten the potency of the program by using professionals.
3. Heighten the potency of rewards by offering actualization awards that actually facilitate a person's personal pursuits.

The Sales Blazer Method—The Simple, Smooth Success of a Sales Blazer

Don, a Sales Blazer, had pulled off another amazing year with a team. That final fiscal year with his previous company, Oracle, caught the attention of a major telecom, which offered him an important leadership role at the company. Don said, "I wouldn't trade my time at Oracle for anything." At the beginning of that year he was saddled, like most successful sales leaders, with increasing quotas. On top of the new high quota, the sales team was experiencing severe pains integrating two major acquisitions. Integrating people from two successful companies, including their cultures and quotas, into an already full set of territories was like doing magic tricks while running a race. Don candidly explained, "Initially, I had little hope of making the huge quota while integrating the new sales forces and all that goes with that. So, what did we do that we hadn't already been doing? Eight things.

"First, we got every distraction out of the way that we could. Second, we spent time with each salesperson and channel partner to get his or her whole commitment. Third, we placed some competitive bets and worked key prospect accounts. Fourth, wherever possible, we focused salespeople and channel partners on opportunities they were best equipped to win. Fifth, we had to make specific assignments so nothing fell through the cracks. Sixth, I had to coach them through some difficult things, and be the kind of leader the challenge deserved. Seventh, we adjusted along the way. As a result, not only did we make the number, we overachieved. We reached 112 percent on a quota that was well into the tens of millions, which equated to a staggering amount of real dollar growth. After the success, we celebrated and rewarded each individual." What Don described about his heroic growth in revenue was in essence what Sales Blazers described before it was captured and put into words.

You have now learned the Sales Blazer Method—the eight common, critical steps to create growth in revenue. Together we have gained a vision of what it takes to force revenue change. If you already have a basic sales process in place but still need to change revenue direction, use the Sales Blazer Method to add an advanced dimension of growth. The eight strategies are the advice you would get from sales leaders who have done the same thing you need to do—employed strategies to rapidly improve growth of your already outstanding results. The strategies were presented in a framework you can repeat—the Sales Blazer Method.

THE ORIGINAL PROMISE

At the beginning of this book, I promised you an action plan that wouldn't take any more time than you currently spend. To summarize, let's explore this bold claim and see whether it is true, and whether the Sales Blazer Method is a different approach to what you already do, and not an entirely new set of tasks.

To recall the strategies in the field, remember how they fit together—three chapters on each side that bookend the middle two. The first three strategies sharpened your ability to *prepare* and use information that really matters. The next two strategies, in Chapters 4 and 5, described how to *engage* a flexible team. The other bookend, the final three strategies, helped you *lead* better. So, how do we put the whole framework of the Sales Blazer Method into a new way of thinking instead of a large, new task list? Something has happened to you by reading this book that you may not yet realize. You will constantly and forever be reminded of eight very important sales lessons. Let's take a look at them.

- *Start with a Clean Bill of Health* by not just sympathizing but by sorting through complaints and resolving only issues that are hampering growth. Every time you hear the often-quoted advice to "see your doctor first," you'll be reminded of Judy. You'll be reminded that issues change, and that what might have been a seemingly normal issue can occasionally drag down the performance of an entire team. All that is required is to remedy such situations before they take root—to take the field's blood pressure, your own or the client's, every few months or so—and listen carefully for issues that distract deeply or broadly—then fix them. This strategy is first in the process because the primary act of a Sales Blazer is to remove obstacles from the path to increasing revenue. Checking on and cleaning things up prevents your efforts in other areas from being obliterated before you even start.
- *Spark a Performance Pursuit* by replacing the senseless catch-up conversations at lunch with direct, appropriate, personal conversations about pursuits and ambitions. Each time you hear about horses or Chichen Itza, you'll recall Chaquita. You'll be reminded to get to know each person in a way that helps you champion his or her personal success. This is the positive place to start, because if you don't know what moves or doesn't move those you're trying to engage as a team, you won't be able to achieve results.
- *Get the Express Pass* to win key, strategic prospects by accelerating the homework you and your team are already expected to do. Every time you hear of an investigative journalist or a theme park, you'll be reminded to get the express pass. You'll remember to encourage performers to make the homework more efficient and to get the basics up front in order to acquire the real story about financial impact as soon as possi-

ble. Use what you learn from your homework to develop a genuine and influential relationship with contacts at strategic accounts. Get to know what will move your prospects and flex your team to help prospects take the next step.

- *Play Your Depth Chart* to position your team to fit their contacts at key opportunities, and, as a result, beat competitors for accounts. From now on, you will be reminded to use all the talent on your team in the right way every time you see a football highlight on the news. Instead of thinking about territories individually, apply your new knowledge about your colleagues' skills to the opportunities and the competition to win. Take that extra moment to consider whether a rep, a support person, or anyone or anything else could add the resource needed to help increase or close important sales.

- *Activate Expectations* by adding relevant specifics to expectations you have already set. Every fad-diet infomercial you click through from now on will remind you to "get real" with sales activities you expect to take place. You can ensure that everyone directly and undeniably contributes to closes in the sales cycle. Activate these particular expectations by offering specific rewards, even if they are small. This will make teamwork predictable and part of the norm in the office—and it will gain you respect.

- *Coach Like a Professional* by being honorable and creating a motivational setting to drive success in all situations. Every scene of Gatorade being poured on a coach will now remind you that there is good reason for highlight reels of players, but the team attributes a big win to the coach. To be honorable is a goal that requires a new set of decisions about what you say and what you do every day. Being an honorable leader means being worthy of high respect, having a positive frame of mind, and making a commitment to get out in the field and hone skills. Lead the charge effectively out in the field and offer feedback.

- *RSVP Feedback* is a way of fine-tuning strengths and reducing mistakes. From today forward, you'll be reminded of how you should give feedback every time you receive an RSVP invitation in the mail. Before letting the words of reaction come out of your mouth, decide whether they should be offered at all. If the time is right for feedback, make it appropriately constructive or, in rare cases, negative. Deliver it smoothly and without hesitation. Request that the salesperson briefly follow up with you (RSVP) following the future success you've described.

- *Heighten Reward Potency* by remembering that it was the salesperson who succeeded, and he or she is who we're celebrating. When you see a sailboat, remember that people have deep, unique passions. Honor the salesperson in appropriate, personal, and motivating ways. This may take a little more thought than you're used to giving to rewards, but hopefully most of the work has already been done (as we've progressed through the chapters). You will maximize your effect by enlisting experts to help you with your rewards program.

SALES BLAZER RESULTS

The Sales Blazer Method is a new approach to the things you do already. If you adopt this better leadership framework and lead with the Sales Blazer Method, you will create revenue growth.

After isolating the secrets of great sales leadership and throwing out extreme successes that involved more than leadership, it is clear that these strategies can have a significant financial impact. As shown in Figure 9.1, the difference in terms of numbers is about 5 percent revenue growth for the norm versus 31 percent for Sales Blazers. That said, as telling as the quotes and the change in revenue are, the difference in attitude, personal approach, and communication is even more inspiring.

Top sales leaders can implement this advanced framework to help people in management positions and aspiring reps influence teams and clients for improved revenue. The Sales Blazer Method creates a growth culture within your organization. Salespeople who use it to direct their teams will outperform their counterparts. Top leaders who share these strategies with the entire sales force will affect the margin of performance. In either case, the informal or formal leader is the pivotal individual who must practice the Sales Blazer Method.

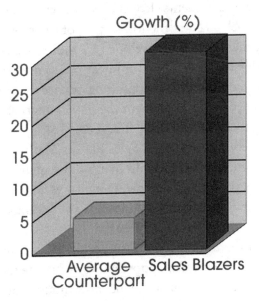

Figure 9.1 Sales Blazer Sales Growth

Without exception, the most valuable feedback I received during the process of preparing this book came from the toughest of top sales leaders who had also been outstanding salespeople. John McVeigh is an example. I asked this Sales Blazer, a former hockey player who in his time literally didn't pull any punches, what he would demand of the Sales Blazers Method.

John said, "I'm part of the most impatient audience in the world—sales leaders. You better cut to the chase and tell me exactly how these strategies are implemented to deliver results, because at the end of the day I don't have time for anything that doesn't deliver results."

I asked Kevin Salmon, a respected sales mentor and leader, the same question. Kevin said, "Give me a one-pager on how this is implemented and how it delivers results."

These two comments led me to develop the Revenue Growth Model. I laid at the foundation of the model a proven consulting methodology, developed by the respected recognition, leadership, and communications consultant Gary Beckstrand along with the consulting services group at O.C. Tanner Company. To implement the model internally, let's discuss it as it is shown in Figure 9.2.

The first component is the Sales Blazers Method—the eight strategies for growth leadership that build sequentially on one another. The baseline for implementation is to measure these abilities in appropriate detail and assess the findings for opportunities to increase sales performance.

Based on the findings of measurement and assessment, plan initiatives to seize growth opportunities. Train the sales force to improve preparation, engagement, and thoughtful leadership using the tools we have learned in the eight strategies. Give

Revenue Growth Model
Eight Strategies for Leading Sales Growth

Strategies

Prepare
1. Start with a Clean Bill of Health: Remove Distractions
2. Spark a Performance Pursuit: Engage Performers
3. Get the Express Pass: Gain Key Information

Engage
4. Play Your Depth Chart: Leverage Talent
5. Activate Expectations: Focus Activity

Lead
6. Coach Like a Professional: Offer Expertise
7. RSVP Feedback: Guide to Success
8. Heighten Reward Potency: Recognize Success

Business Results

Leadership Influence
▼

Client & Sales Performance
- More selling time
- Engaged reps & teams
- Enhanced advisory role
- Greater rewards

▼
Revenue Growth

Professional Services

Measure | Assess | Design | Train | Execute | Measure

Sales Blazers Method®

Prepare · Engage · Lead

Figure 9.2 Revenue Growth Model

267

assistance, tools, milestones to frontline leaders and salespeople so that they can improve with the least amount of distraction from selling during execution.

Finally, measure results to determine progress. When effective leadership behaviors are adopted by a consultative sales team, results will follow. Success requires and deserves reward to keep the momentum; reward those that show measured improvement. Expect to see selling time go up, with teams engaged in mutual success and perceived by clients in an advisory role. With improved results, improved rewards show appreciation and revenue growth is achieved.

The Revenue Growth Model is an execution map for applying the Sales Blazers Method. In between measures, you will be able to clear up any severe problems that are hampering performance. As you continue to monitor your progress, you will discover the path to the most powerful motivators for each salesperson and customer. You will be able to discover the strategies of your competitors early, and you will be able to organize flexibly to beat them. Your people will be put in positions to succeed, and they will understand the consequences clearly. As you reward their individual successes, you will also ensure that their future successes will be greater. The end result? Your team will exude leadership influence. A new force of leadership-minded salespeople will spend more time selling. Reps and teams will engage in the work and demonstrate cooperation as never before. Clients and teammates will see you as a trusted advisor, and the rewards will be meaningful. The final result will be that your team will generate an increased sales trajectory—and you will blaze through your sales goals.

Notes

Introduction

4   *"They didn't believe it was possible."* Bo Scott, manuscript review interview notes, September 12, 2006.

5   *"Last year's big success sure fades fast."* Dan Nelson, research interview by author, transcript, p. 15, May 12, 2006.

6   *"... sometimes last year's big success is this year's fiercest rival."* Kevin Salmon, research interview by author, notes, p. 2, April 5, 2006.

Strategy 1

16   *"Fixing the right small problems can have a tremendous impact on productivity."* Tina Zitting, research interview by author, manuscript review notes, August 10, 2006.

16   *The following events, based on several true stories* ... See Susan Schindehette, "The Haunting Last Days of Jim Henson," *People*, June 18, 1990, pp. 88–96. See also Lois M. Collins and Elaine Jarvik, "Still Lisa: Strep Infection Turned Childbirth into Battle to Survive," *Deseret Morning News* [Salt Lake City, UT], Sunday, March 12, 2006.

18   *More than one-quarter of children carry it* ... Marc Lukasiak and Melanie Finnigan, "Children's Hospital Offers Parents Tips to Keep Children Strep-Free During Peak Months," *Children's Hospital of Pittsburgh*, December 15, 2006, http://www.chp.edu/pressroom/newsrelease325.php

22   *... $25,000 medical expense instead of on the next sale.* Research observation I166043159, meeting with author, September 10, 2006; and Research observation I163488675, discussion with author, September 11, 2006.

23   *... observation of businesspeople has shown that all managers have blind spots* ... See J. Luft and H. Ingham, "The Johari Window, a Graphic Model of Interpersonal Awareness," *Proceedings of the Western Training Laboratory in Group Development* (Los Angeles: UCLA, 1955).

25   *Hygiene factors hamper motivation and prevent improving results.* See Fredrick Herzberg, Bernard Mausner, and Barbara B. Snyderman, *The Motivation to Work* (New York: Wiley, 1959).

27   *"How you identify, acknowledge, and pursue a quick resolution is key ..."* Tim Scott, manuscript review interview notes, September 10, 2006.

27   *"Instead of leading, the CEO communicated how he really felt ..."* Research observation I159869823, meetings with author, 2006.

28   *A Sales Blazer detects teamwork issues* ... Survey response 163488675, Sales Leadership Survey by author (respondents' names of this portion of the research have been fictionalized and company names removed to protect confidentiality), October 10, 2005.

29   *"I'd put up with all the other annoying things ..."* Research
interview I157953960, anonymous interview of "Joan" and
"Jane" in New York cab, October 10, 2004.

30   *"But when you don't hear one single complaint ..."* Research
interview I158166834, interview of anonymous sales vice president, Notes, p. 1, May 12, 2006.

31   *"We really want to work hard with them."* Multiple observations, Sales Leadership Survey by author, October 10, 2005.

32   *"Kari's willingness ..."* Meredith Moll, telephone interview by
author, September 2007.

33   *"We have sustained this for three years."* Michael Greenbaum
and employees of CyraCom International, telephone conversations and Sales Leadership Survey by author, October
2005–August 2007.

34   *"He's not just our leader ..."* Angela Au and employee of AMR,
telephone conversations and Sales Leadership Survey by author,
October 2005–August 2007.

34   *Gary's team increased their sales ...* Gary West, telephone conversations and e-mail, August 2007.

39   *"... l eaders who succeeded were those who actively tried to get
things out of my way ..."* Jon Roderick and Brian McKaig, interviews, telephone conversations, and e-mail by author, transcript,
p. 24, October 2005–August 2007.

Strategy 2

43   *"Trust is key ..."* Tim Treu, meetings with author, September
2007.

43   *"... free agents ..."* Daniel H. Pink, "Free Agent Nation,"
FastCompany, December 1997/January 1998, p. 131.

43   *"... 54 percent of today's workers have five or fewer years left ..."*
Alison T. Touhey, "The Shift Away from Defined Benefit Plans,"

FDIC Outlook, Spring 2006, www.fdic.gov/bank/analytical/regional/ro20061q/na/2006_spring02. See also Elissa Tucker, Tina Kao, and Nidhi Verma, "Next-Generation Talent Management: Insights on How Workforce Trends Are Changing the Face of Talent Management," Hewitt Associates, www.workinfo.com/free/Downloads/NextGeneration.pdf.

43   *... new positions made available by retiring baby boomers* ... Jeffery A. Joerres, *Manpower Talent Shortage Survey*, February 21, 2006, www.ca.manpower.com/cacom/PressRelease.jsp?id=58&articleid=136&language=en.

44   *Fifty percent of employees spend part of their day actively looking* ... Harris Interactive and Spherion Corporation, *Emerging Workforce Study*, November 2005, www.spherion.com/press/releases/2005/Emerging_Workforce.jsp. See also *Confronting the Chemical Industry Brain Drain*, Accenture Institute for Strategic Change, April 2002.

44   *... they stay in the workforce longer* ... "The Ageing Workforce: Turning Boomers into Boomerangs," *The Economist*, February 16, 2006, www.economist.com/business/displaystory.cfm?story_id=5519033. See also Ian Davis and Elizabeth Stephenson, "Ten Trends to Watch in 2006," *The McKinsey Quarterly*, January 2006, p. 3, www.zilliant.com/downloads/McKinsey_Top10Trends2006.pdf.

44   *"... opportunities for personal growth ..."* McKinsey & Company, "Making a Market in Talent." *The McKinsey Quarterly*, Visitor Edition, May 3, 2006, www.mckinseyquarterly.com/article_abstract_visitor.aspx?ar=1765&L2=18&L3=31. See also Tim Hindel, "The New Organisation," *The Economist*, January 19, 2006, www.microsoft.com/business/peopleready/news/economist/neworg.mspx.

45   *... employees rank personal "growth" and "earnings potential" second* ... Harris Interactive, "Emerging Workforce Study," Spherion Corporation Study, November 2005; and TCG, primary research for OC Tanner strategy discussion, 2006.

45   *... management innovations ...* See the McKinsey Group, "What's Right with the US Economy," *The McKinsey Quarterly*, Visitor Edition, 3 May 2006, www.mckinseyquarterly.com/article_abstract_visitor.aspx?ar=1635&L2=1&L3=106. See also Ian Davis and Elizabeth Stephenson, "Ten Trends to Watch in 2006," *The McKinsey Quarterly*, January 2006, p. 3, www.zilliant.com/downloads/McKinsey_Top10Trends2006.pdf; and Elissa Tucker, Tina Kao, and Nidhi Verma, "Next-Generation Talent Management: Insights on How Workforce Trends Are Changing the Face of Talent Management," Hewitt Associates, www.workinfo.com/free/Downloads/NextGeneration.pdf.

46   *"... we have all the thoroughbreds in place."* Mark Ludwig, sales management meeting with author, April 5, 2004.

50   *"It's great to get a horse that goes out and gets the fast times."* Terry Groom, telephone interview with author, transcript, p. 5, April 27, 2006.

50   *"... barrel racers refer to the last leg as going home ..."* Debbie Foley, telephone interview with author, transcript, p. 2, April 27, 2006.

51   *"... the ranch is such a great place for them."* Loren Moench, telephone interview with author, transcript, p. 9, 27 April 2006.

51   *... if they're also pursuing what's most important to them.* See Douglas McGregor, *The Human Side of Enterprise* (New York: McGraw-Hill, 1960).

52   *"... to understand and assist me in my personal goals for success in life."* Sharon Andersen and anonymous salesperson, telephone interviews and Sales Leadership Survey by author, notes, January–September 2007.

52   *Famous behavioral scientist Abraham Maslow...* Abraham Maslow, "A Theory of Human Motivation," *Psychological Review*, 50 (1943): 370–396.

60   *His accelerated growth was "significant" to his company's success.* Multiple observations, Sales Leadership Survey by author, October 10, 2005.

61 *"... from this perspective, progress is limitless."* Research observation 155625566, Sales Leadership Survey by author, October
10, 2005.

61 *Some progressive companies have set up talent markets ...* See the
McKinsey Group, "Making a Market in Talent," *The McKinsey
Quarterly,* Visitor Edition, May 3, 2006, www.mckinseyquarterly
.com/article_abstract_visitor.aspx?ar= 1635&L2=1&L3=106.

63 *"... she needs to get that number up."* Wynn (last name
unknown), telephone conversation on shuttle next to author,
notes p. 1, November 18, 2004.

64 *"... the great companies are embracing the personal approach."*
Jon Roderick, research interview by author, transcript, p. 25,
March 2, 2006.

65 *Herbert Kelman ...* Herbert C. Kelman and V. Lee Hamilton,
Crimes of Obedience (New Haven and London: Yale University
Press, 1989), pp. 79–113. See also Mark Oborne/Petrous,
Farmington and Bountiful, Utah, Brideless Leadership discussion
and workshop, 2006.

69 *"... learn what makes people tick ..."* Research observation
155619704, Sales Leadership Survey by author, October 10,
2005.

69 *"... one hour per direct report per month discussing personal and
career goals."* Bo Scott, manuscript review interview notes,
September 12, 2006.

72 *"... we talk about my assignments ..."* Tina Zitting, research
interview and meeting observed by author, transcript, pp. 1–2,
March 5 and April 27, 2006.

72 *"I would move mountains for her ..."* Mandi Kerr, conversation
with author, Tina Zitting notes, p. 2, March 10, 2006.

74 *"... we're the ones who helped him see the possibility."* Bo Scott,
manuscript review interview notes, June 2007.

Strategy 3

81   *"... you lose the ability to play ..."* Research observation
I159869823, research interview by author, transcript, p. 16, May
7, 2006.

83   *... strategic accounts ...* Research observation I158379708,
telephone interview by author, notes, p. 1, September 28, 2005.

85   *"... surroundings, and resources available ..."* Tim Scott, research
interviews by author, notes, p. 2, October 2005–June 2007.

93   *"... you care about their success ..."* Tom Rosato, research interviews by author, transcript, September 2007.

95   *She felt gratified ...* Scott Jensen, conversations and manuscript
reviews with author, transcript, September 2007.

96   *"The reason we selected you ..."* Kevin Salmon, research interviews and work with author, review sheet, June 29, 2006.

96   *"You have to understand the real pain ..."* Darin Gilson, meetings with author, notes, p. 1, August, 18, 2005.

97   *"The specifics are shocking."* IRE, "2005 IRE Award Winners,"
IRE.org: Complete List of 2005 IRE Award Winners and Finalists
page, www.ire.org/contest/05winners.html#finalists.

97   *"I guess our goals really are similar."* John Maines, telephone
interviews by author, transcript and notes, pp. 11–15, May 10,
2006.

101 *... $6 million revenue into an astounding $100 million.* Dan
Nelson, research interview by author, transcript, p. 6, May 12,
2006.

106 *"They better really know ..."* Glenn Seninger, lunch meeting
with author, notes, June 8, 2004.

106 *"Salespeople are expected to develop a long-term relationship ..."*
Chris Williams, telephone interviews with author, notes, p. 1,
June 9, 2004.

108   *"You have to know how you can provide every value ..."* Tim Scott, research interviews by author, transcript, October 2005–June 2007.

112   *"people prefer to buy from people they like ..."* Tom Rosato, research interviews by author, transcript, September 2007.

113   *"... my brother's ligament ..."* Dan Nelson, research interview by author, transcript, p. 6, May 12, 2006.

114   *"He's a hard worker ..."* Research observation 154454394, Sales Leadership Survey by author, October 10, 2005.

116   *"... bring the right resources to bear for each."* Kevin Salmon, research interview by author, review sheet, June 29, 2006.

117   *"Revenue had been falling monthly ..."* Michael Fox, telephone interviews by author, transcript, July–September 2007.

Strategy 4

125   *"We also need new urgency ..."* Research observation I163488675, conversations with author, notes, June–August 2006.

126   *"... getting the right people on the bus ..."* Jim Collins, *Good to Great* (New York: HarperCollins, 2001), p. 41.

126   *"She found a way to utilize people's talents ..."* Multiple observations, Sales Leadership Survey by author, October 10, 2005.

127   *... assigning people work with which they have experience ...* See Clayton E. Tucker-Ladd, "Chapter 4: Behavior, Motivation and Self-Control (Edward Thorndike)," www.psychologicalselfhelp .org/Chapter4.pdf.

128   *His marshaling of the right people ...* Hal Hodges, work and meetings with author, transcript, September 2007.

128   *"... Eagle Scout medallion."* Scott Crawford, meetings and telephone interviews with author, transcript, September 2007.

132   *Coach Mark Panella is the person* … Mark Panella, telephone interview with author, notes, pp. 8–10, May 18, 2006.

137   *"When I first came here, people were assigned stringent boundaries …"* Tina Zitting, research interview and meeting observed by author, transcript, pp. 1–2, March 5 and April 27 2006.

138   *"It's not always about the top performer …"* Kevin Salmon, research interview by author, review sheet, June 29, 2006.

138   *"… you reach out to any specialist who can help you."* Kim Purcell, conversations and telephone interviews with author, transcript, September 2007.

140   *"… too much movement can paralyze results."* Tim Scott, research interview by author, notes, p. 2, October 12, 2005.

141   *"… our prospects like to see us as experts."* James Soto, multiple meetings with author, notes, pp. 1–2, January 2006.

142   *"… bring talent and information from anywhere …"* Research observation I157528213, Sales Leadership Survey by author, October 10, 2005.

148   *"… if situations come up that require some changes, they will be made …"* Jon Roderick, research interview by author, transcript, p. 24, March 2, 2006.

149   *"People adjusted and now they actually like it."* Don Ameche, telephone interview with author, notes, p. 1, October 5, 2005.

150   *"But it's important to adjust …"* Kevin Salmon, research interview by author, review sheet, June 29, 2006.

150   *"… if they know it's worth their time …"* Tina Zitting, research interview and meeting observed by author, transcript, pp. 1–2, March 5 and April 27, 2006.

Strategy 5

157   *"You have to reward people more than once a year …"* Multiple observations, Sales Leadership Survey by author, October 10, 2005.

158   "... he would help us identify the exact steps we needed ..." Lisa Mott, e-mail to author, August 17, 2007; and salesperson for Sprint, Sales Leadership Survey by author, October 10, 2005.

158   "We find a way to assign and reward things ..." Observation I158379708, telephone interview by author, notes, p. 1, September 28, 2005; and multiple sales calls, 2004–2005.

159   "We broke our strategy down ..." Bo Scott, manuscript review interview notes, September 12, 2006.

161   "... to the extent I can specifically refine expectations ..." Blake Hawkes, meetings and telephone conversation with author, transcript, August 2007.

163   B. F. Skinner, a famous motivational psychologist ... See B. F. Skinner, The Behavior of Organisms: An Experimental Analysis (New York: Appleton-Century, 1938); and C. B. Fester and B. F. Skinner, Schedules of Reinforcement (New York: Appleton Century Croft, 1957).

163   ... (RIC). Kim Smithson, meetings with author quoting Skinner, 2005.

164   ... punishment rarely motivates long-term results. Jay Kimiecik, "Outcome versus Performance Goals," HumanKinetics.com, Human Kinetics Publishers, www.humankinetics.com/products/showexcerpt.cfm?excerpt_id=3480. See also Victor H. Vroom, Work and Motivation (New York: Wiley, 1964); Edward Lawler, Motivation in Work Organizations (Monterey, CA: Brooks/Cole, 1973); Edward Vockell, Educational Psychology: A Practical Approach, http://education.calumet.purdue.edu/Vockell/EdPsyBook; Etienne Benson, "Rehabilitate or Punish?," APA Online: Monitor on Psychology, 34 (July/August 2003): 46; Douglas McGregor, The Human Side of Enterprise (New York: McGraw-Hill, 1960).

165   Leadership should design policies ... Elissa Tucker, Tina Kao, and Nidhi Verma, "Next-Generation Talent Management: Insights on How Workforce Trends Are Changing the Face of

Talent Management," Hewitt Associates, www.workinfo.com/ free/Downloads/NextGeneration.pdf.

166   *Self-efficacy* ... Albert Bandura, "Self-efficacy," In V. S. Ramachaudran (ed.), *Encyclopedia of Human Behavio*r, Vol. 4 (New York: Academic Press, 1994), pp. 71–81; reprinted in H. Friedman (ed.), *Encyclopedia of Mental Health* (San Diego, CA: Academic Press, 1998), www.des.emory.edu/mfp/BanEncy.html. See also Victor H. Vroom, *Work and Motivation* (New York: Wiley, 1964).

167   *"Support people are calling salespeople ..."* Observation I158379708, telephone interview by author, notes, p. 1, August 2007.

167   *"Our specific assignments have measurable outcomes ..."* Tim Scott, research interview by author, notes, p. 2, October 12, 2005.

172   *"We simply found the things that really work ..."* Robert Green, research interviews by author, transcript, p. 6, January–June 2007.

173   *Beth gave the staffer the criteria* ... Beth Thornton, telephone conversation with author, notes, April 7, 2004.

174   *"... show us results we can achieve right now."* Doug Christensen, interview by author, notes, p. 1, February 4, 2005.

Strategy 6

179   *"Rah-rah without substance ..."* Bo Scott, manuscript review interview notes, September 12, 2006.

180   *"... he jumped off my bandwagon ..."* Research observation I163488675, conversations with author, notes, June–August 2006.

181   *... a model of honorable behavior* ... Doug Duckworth, work with author, April 2004–January 2005.

181   *... leader ... setting ... action ...* Herbert C. Kelman and V. Lee Hamilton, *Crimes of Obedience* (New Haven and London: Yale University Press, 1989), pp. 79–113.

182   *"... socially disapproved activities."* Ibid., p. 83.

185   *"That's what coaching is all about."* Tim Scott, research interview by author, notes, p. 2, October 12, 2005.

186   *"... they have to be open to coaching ..."* Multiple observations, Sales Leadership Survey by author, October 10, 2005.

186   *David McCullough describes George Washington ...* David McCullough, *1776* (New York: Simon & Schuster, 2005), p. 43.

189   *"... service-oriented approach."* Research observation 154370187, Sales Leadership Survey by author, October 10, 2005.

190   *"And most of all he walks his talk ..."* Debbie Urbanik, conversations, e-mail, and telephone interviews with author, transcript and e-mail, September 2007.

190   *... his respect for people ...* Dianne Piet, meetings and telephone conversations with author, 2004–2007.

191   *"... recommend and ensure solutions proactively ..."* Doug Mercer, meeting with author, transcript, September 21, 2007.

191   *"Respect is an essential part ..."* Research observation 155631863, Sales Leadership Survey by author, October 10, 2005.

192   *"... being near the game and coaching the team in the field ..."* RC Anderson, research interview with author, transcript, p. 2, May 24, 2006.

192   *Kelman's leader, an influencing agent ...* Herbert C. Kelman and V. Lee Hamilton, *Crimes of Obedience* (New Haven and London: Yale University Press, 1989), p. 83.

194   *"I decided things better be bright ..."* Deb Phipps, author's visits and work with associate, organizer notes, June 23, 2004.

194 *"you can't micromanage ..."* Joe Swanholm, Author's visits and work with salesperson, organizer notes, 2004–2005.

196 *Product knowledge alone is not leadership.* Bo Scott, manuscript review interview notes, September 12, 2006.

198 *"I refuse to be seen as just a salesman ..."* Bryan McGrath, conversations, presentation, and work with author, discussions of Bryan's PowerPoint presentation about strategic recognition, 2004–2005.

201 *"... effort and focus they give on the field ..."* Mark Panella, telephone interview with author, notes, pp. 3–4, May 18, 2006.

202 *"... by sharing our philosophy and practices on coaching."* Gail Bedke, meetings with author, notes, September 2007.

Strategy 7

207 *... feedback is the leadership attribute of Sales Blazers that correlates most ...* Correlations of responses to "significance of growth to company," Sales Leadership Survey by author, October 10, 2005.

208 *"... two-way communication."* Multiple observations, Sales Leadership Survey by author, October 10, 2005.

210 *"I make sure I have something more specific to offer ..."* Kelly Phillipps, work and discussions with author, notes, August 2005–November 2007.

212 *"... CEO friend I felt was making a mistake."* Research observation I158592581, discussion with author, notes, August–November 2005.

215 *... consideration turns back to the giver of the feedback.* Alan Bryce, work and discussions with author, notes, August 2007.

218 *"Managers who are too nice ..."* Anonymous sales vice president, discussions with author, June 15, 2005, notes, August–November 2006.

219   *... the client offered a trip to Hawaii ...* Kevin Salmon, conversation with author, review sheet, August 3, 2006.

223   *"Do we have a deal to call each other in three weeks to check in?"* Research observation I158592581, discussion with author, notes, August–November 2005.

224   *"Now they expect feedback."* Kim Robinson, telephone interviews and meetings with author, notes, p. 1, September 13, 2005, and March 2, 2006.

225   *"It became so mechanical that everyone stopped listening."* Anonymous sales vice president, discussions with author, June 15, 2005, notes, August–November 2006.

226   *... they do it now.* Maryann Hammers and Gerhard Gschwandtner, "7 Leadership Qualities of the Best Sales Managers," *Selling Power*, May 2004, p. 63.

227   *"... if you want to talk about it I'll be in next week."* Rulon Horne, meeting with author, August 2007.

Strategy 8

234   *"I'm one of those fanatical sailors."* Robert Baird, meetings with author, e-mail, December 2005 and March 28, 2006.

235   *"Sailing's in my blood."* Wid Warner, telephone interviews, meetings, and sailing with author, transcript, pp. 1–2, May 28–October 2006.

238   *... definition of recognition ... Merriam-Webster's Dictionary* (Springfield, MA: Merriam-Webster, 2002), http://dictionary.reference.com/search?q=recognition#lookup.

239   *"... Wonder trip ..."* Chris Skillings, telephone interviews, work with author, e-mail, and notes, March 2003–2006.

240   *"No matter how small the contribution ..."* Research observation 156832623, Sales Leadership Survey by author, October 10, 2005.

241   *Adrian Gostick and Chester Elton said ...* Adrian Gostick and Chester Elton, *The Carrot Principle* (New York: The Free Press, 2007).

244   *Dennis Conner on the right crew ...* Dennis Conner, quoted at ThinkExist.com, "Dennis Conner quotes," en.thinkexist.com/ quotes/dennis_conner.

244   *"Well-designed programs ..."* Michelle Smith, telephone conversations, 2006. See also Richard E. Clark, Steven J. Condly, and Harold D. Stolovitch for the International Society of Performance Improvement and SITE Foundation, "Incentive, Motivation and Workplace Performance," as quoted in Forum for People Performance, www.performanceforum.org/PFM/whitepaper1 .asp#2, and *Management and Performance Improvement Quarterly*, 16(3) (2003): 46–63.

245   *"Truly motivational programs ..."* Ed Robbins, meetings and telephone conversations, 2005–2007.

247   *"How these incentives express themselves ..."* Bo Scott, manuscript review interview notes, September 12, 2006.

249   *... it's a good idea to get relevant professional advice ...* Christine Kubert, telephone interviews with author, transcript, pp. 1–4, January 2005 and June 1, 2006.

250   *"If you're trying to create a professional bond ..."* Randy Reneer, telephone interviews, work with author, e-mail, and notes, March 2003–2006.

Conclusion

266   *"... I don't have time for anything that doesn't deliver ..."* John McVeigh, meeting and telephone conversation with author, transcript, July–August 2007.

266   *"Give me a one-pager ..."* Kevin Salmon, meeting with author, September 2007.

Index

About the Author

Mark Cook wrote *Sales Blazers* while working as director of sales and marketing for O.C. Tanner, a leading employee performance company. Previously, Cook served as vice president of sales and marketing for Center 7, a provider of system-management technology. He was also the founder and publisher of *Priorities: The Journal of Professional Success* while direc-tor of marketing with Stephen R. Covey's organization, FranklinCovey. Cook holds a bachelor's degree and a master's degree in business with an emphasis in sales and marketing from the David Eccles School of Business at the University of Utah in Salt Lake City.